Algebra 2

LARSON
BOSWELL
KANOLD
STIFF

Applications • Equations • Graphs

Basic Skills Workbook:
Diagnosis and Remediation

The Basic Skills Workbook provides material you can use to
review and practice basic prerequisite skills for Algebra 2.
A diagnostic test is provided to help you determine which
topics in the workbook need to be reviewed.

McDougal Littell
A HOUGHTON MIFFLIN COMPANY
Evanston, Illinois • Boston • Dallas

Contents

Diagnostic Test

For use before Topic 1

Operations with Integers (Topic 1, Lesson 1, pages 1–7)

Evaluate the expression.

1. $-11 + 6$ **2.** $-7 - 19$ **3.** $9(-9)$

4. $42 \div (-6)$ **5.** $5(9 - 15)$ **6.** $\dfrac{30 - 6}{2 \cdot 4^2 - 20}$

Operations with Rational Numbers (Topic 1, Lesson 2, pages 8–13)

Evaluate the expression. Write your answer in simplest form.

7. $\dfrac{3}{8} + \dfrac{7}{8}$ **8.** $\dfrac{2}{3} - \dfrac{5}{12}$ **9.** $12.65 - 9.899$

10. $\dfrac{6}{9} \times \dfrac{12}{14}$ **11.** $\dfrac{18}{7} \div \dfrac{6}{14}$

12. 17.5×3.65 **13.** $\left(\dfrac{2}{9} + \dfrac{5}{6}\right) - \dfrac{1}{3}$

Square Root Concepts (Topic 1, Lesson 3, pages 14–18)

Evaluate the expression.

14. $\sqrt{36}$ **15.** $\pm\sqrt{16}$ **16.** $-2\sqrt{81}$

Approximate the square root.

17. $\sqrt{52}$ **18.** $-\sqrt{108}$ **19.** $\sqrt{80}$

Simplifying Square Roots (Topic 1, Lesson 4, pages 19–23)

Simplify the expression. Rationalize the denominator when necessary.

20. $\sqrt{28}$ **21.** $\sqrt{6} \cdot \sqrt{12}$ **22.** $3\sqrt{\dfrac{7}{12}}$

23. $3\sqrt{6} - 8\sqrt{6}$ **24.** $\sqrt{128} + \sqrt{50}$ **25.** $\sqrt{3} \cdot \sqrt{6} - \sqrt{18}$

Evaluating Expressions (Topic 2, Lesson 1, pages 25–29)

Write a variable expression for the verbal phrase.

26. 36 divided by x **27.** x minus 19

28. 45 plus x **29.** -8 times x

1. _____
2. _____
3. _____
4. _____
5. _____
6. _____
7. _____
8. _____
9. _____
10. _____
11. _____
12. _____
13. _____
14. _____
15. _____
16. _____
17. _____
18. _____
19. _____
20. _____
21. _____
22. _____
23. _____
24. _____
25. _____
26. _____
27. _____
28. _____
29. _____

DIAGNOSTIC TEST **CONTINUED**

Diagnostic Test
For use before Topic 1

Evaluate the expression for the given value of the variable.

30. $-6x$ when $x = -9$

31. $\dfrac{y}{7}$ when $y = -49$

Simplifying Expressions (Topic 2, Lesson 2, pages 30–34)

Simplify the expression.

32. $-28 + 13x + 16$

33. $10x - (-3x + 5)$

34. $(2y^2 - 9y + 16) - (5y^2 + 3y - 3)$

35. $(6x^2 + 7x + 1) + (-2x^2 - 8)$

36. $4y(2 - y) + 3y^2$

37. $-7x + 8(-2x + 5)$

Properties of Powers (Topic 2, Lesson 3, pages 35–39)

Evaluate the expression.

38. $3^3 \cdot 3^2$

39. $\left(\dfrac{1}{2}\right)^{-1}$

40. $\dfrac{5^6}{5^4}$

Simplify the expression. The simplified expression should have no negative exponents.

41. $\dfrac{4x^8}{6x^{-5}}$

42. $(3x \cdot x^3)^{-2}$

43. $(12xy)^0(x^2y^4)^5$

Simplifying Expressions with Powers (Topic 2, Lesson 4, pages 40–44)

Simplify the product.

44. $(2x)(3x^3 - 5x)$

45. $(6xy^2)(-8x + 9y)$

46. $\dfrac{x^2y}{3y^3x^3} \cdot \dfrac{18x^4y^2}{xy^6}$

47. $\dfrac{2x^{-2}y}{3y^{-3}x^2} \cdot \dfrac{3x^4}{8y^{-2}}$

Evaluate the expression. Write the result in scientific notation.

48. $(3 \times 10^3) \cdot (9 \times 10^{-2})$

49. $\dfrac{2.4 \times 10^{-2}}{1.2 \times 10^{-5}}$

Solving Equations (Topic 3, Lesson 1, pages 46–51)

State the inverse.

50. Subtract 21

51. Divide by -6

52. Multiply by 14

Solve the equation.

53. $x - 18 = -3$

54. $\dfrac{2}{3}x = 18$

55. $5x - 3 = 12$

| 30. _____ |
| 31. _____ |
| 32. _____ |
| 33. _____ |
| 34. _____ |
| 35. _____ |
| 36. _____ |
| 37. _____ |
| 38. _____ |
| 39. _____ |
| 40. _____ |
| 41. _____ |
| 42. _____ |
| 43. _____ |
| 44. _____ |
| 45. _____ |
| 46. _____ |
| 47. _____ |
| 48. _____ |
| 49. _____ |
| 50. _____ |
| 51. _____ |
| 52. _____ |
| 53. _____ |
| 54. _____ |
| 55. _____ |

Algebra 2
Basic Skills Workbook : Diagnosis and Remediation

Diagnostic Test

For use before Topic 1

Solving Inequalities (Topic 3, Lesson 2, pages 52–57)

Solve the inequality.

56. $x + 4 < 18$ **57.** $-9 \geq 5 + x$ **58.** $-8x \leq 40$

59. $\dfrac{x}{12} > -\dfrac{1}{3}$ **60.** $6 < -5x + 11$ **61.** $9 \leq \dfrac{2}{3}x - 3$

Solving Multi-Step Equations and Inequalities
(Topic 3, Lesson 3, pages 58–63)

Solve the equation if possible.

62. $16x + 24 = 7(x + 6)$ **63.** $-4(2x - 1) = 3 - 8x$

64. $5(2x - 3) = -15 + 10x$ **65.** $-6x^2 = -216$

Solve the inequality.

66. $3(4x - 5) < -3x$ **67.** $-6 - x \geq -7x + 12$

68. $8(2 - x) \leq -4(x - 5)$

Writing and Solving Proportions (Topic 3, Lesson 4, pages 64–69)

Solve the proportion.

69. $\dfrac{x}{8} = \dfrac{3}{12}$ **70.** $\dfrac{x + 6}{4} = \dfrac{-4x}{16}$ **71.** $\dfrac{2}{3} = \dfrac{x + 7}{3x}$

In Exercises 72 and 73, pairs of similar triangles are shown. Find the missing lengths of sides.

72.

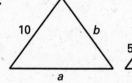

73.

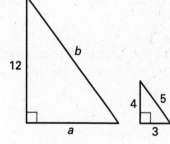

56.	_____
57.	_____
58.	_____
59.	_____
60.	_____
61.	_____
62.	_____
63.	_____
64.	_____
65.	_____
66.	_____
67.	_____
68.	_____
69.	_____
70.	_____
71.	_____
72. *a* =	_____
b =	_____
73. *a* =	_____
b =	_____

Algebra 2
Basic Skills Workbook: Diagnosis and Remediation

NAME _____ DATE _____

Diagnostic Test

For use before Topic 1

Plotting Points (Topic 4, Lesson 1, pages 71–75)

Write the ordered pairs that correspond to the points labeled *A, B, C,* and *D* in the coordinate plane.

74.

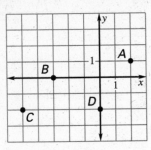

75.

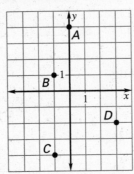

Plot the ordered pair in a coordinate plane and tell whether it is in Quadrant 1, Quadrant 2, Quadrant 3, or Quadrant 4.

76. $(-3, 2)$

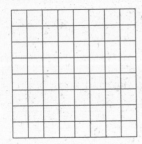

77. $(5, -1)$

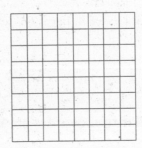

Slope-Intercept Form of a Linear Equation
(Topic 4, Lesson 2, pages 76–80)

Find the slope and *y*-intercept of the graph of the equation.

78. $y = -2x + 7$ **79.** $3x + 6y = 12$ **80.** $y = \dfrac{2x + 7}{14}$

Graph the equation.

81. $y = x + 3$

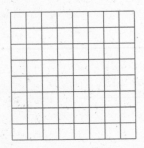

82. $y = -2x + 1$

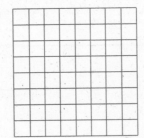

74. A _____

   B _____

   C _____

   D _____

75. A _____

   B _____

   C _____

   D _____

76. Plot at left _____

   Quadrant: _____

77. Plot at left _____

   Quadrant: _____

78. _____

   _____

79. _____

   _____

80. _____

   _____

81. Use graph at left.

82. Use graph at left.

Algebra 2
Basic Skills Workbook : Diagnosis and Remediation

Diagnostic Test

For use before Topic 1

Quick Graphs Using Intercepts (Topic 4, Lesson 3, pages 81–84)

Find the *x*-intercept and the *y*-intercept of the line. Graph the equation. Label the points where the line crosses the axes.

83. $y = x - 5$

84. $6x + 2y = -12$

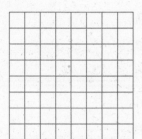

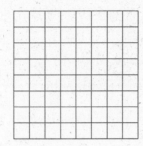

Nonlinear Equations (Topic 4, Lesson 4, pages 85–89)

Sketch the graph of the function. Label the vertex.

85. $y = 3x^2$

86. $y = x^2 + 4x - 2$

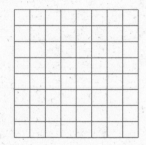

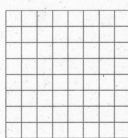

Sketch the graph of the function.

87. $y = |x|$

88. $y = |x - 3|$

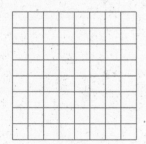

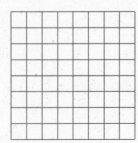

Common Monomial Factors (Topic 5, Lesson 1, pages 91–95)

Find the greatest common factor and factor it out of the expression.

89. $-4x^3 - 20x^2 + 16x$

90. $15x^5 - 10x^4 + 5x^2$

91. $3x^5y^2 - 21x^2y^7$

92. $-2x^2y^3 + 7xy^7$

83. _____

_____

Use graph at left. ____

84. _____

_____

Use graph at left. ____

85. Use graph at left. ____

86. Use graph at left. ____

87. Use graph at left. ____

88. Use graph at left. ____

89. _____

90. _____

91. _____

92. _____

DIAGNOSTIC
TEST

CONTINUED

NAME _____ DATE _____

Diagnostic Test

For use before Topic 1

Factoring $x^2 + bx + c$ (Topic 5, Lesson 2, pages 96–100)

Factor the trinomial.

93. $x^2 + 6x + 9$ **94.** $x^2 - 12x + 36$

95. $x^2 - 2x - 24$ **96.** $x^2 + 2x - 35$

Factoring $ax^2 + bx + c$ (Topic 5, Lesson 3, pages 101–105)

Factor the trinomial.

97. $2x^2 + x - 6$ **98.** $9x^2 + 24x + 16$

99. $3x^2 - 17x - 56$ **100.** $12x^2 + 46x - 36$

Factoring Special Cases (Topic 5, Lesson 4, pages 106–110)

Factor the expression.

101. $9x^2 - 81$ **102.** $x^2 + 20x + 100$ **103.** $121 - x^2$

Factor the expression completely.

104. $x^4 - 9x^2$ **105.** $x^3 + 11x^2 + 28x$

106. $-3x^3 - 15x^2 - 12x$ **107.** $8x^3 - 3x^2 + 16x - 6$

93. _____

94. _____

95. _____

96. _____

97. _____

98. _____

99. _____

100. _____

101. _____

102. _____

103. _____

104. _____

105. _____

106. _____

107. _____

LESSON 1.1

Operations with Integers

GOAL Add, subtract, multiply, and divide integers.

Terms to Know	*Example/Illustration*
Integer any number that is a positive or negative whole number or zero (On a horizontal number line, the negative integers are to the left of 0 and the positive integers are to the right of 0.)	. . . $-4, -3, -2, -1, 0, 1, 2, 3, 4,$ . . . Negative Zero Positive integers ↓ integers -3 -2 -1 0 1 2 3
Opposites two numbers whose sum is zero	-3 and 3 are opposites because $-3 + 3 = 0$
Absolute value on a number line, the distance from the number to 0 (The symbol $|x|$ is read "the absolute value of x.")	⊢2 units⊦2 units⊣ -3 -2 -1 0 1 2 3 $|-2| = 2$ and $|2| = 2$

Understanding the Main Ideas

Addition of integers can be modeled with movements on a number line. For example:

$$-1 + 2 = 1 \qquad\qquad 1 + (-2) = -1 \qquad\qquad -1 + (-2) = -3$$

$-2\ -1\ \ 0\ \ 1\ \ 2$ $\qquad\qquad$ $-2\ -1\ \ 0\ \ 1\ \ 2$ $\qquad\qquad$ $-4\ -3\ -2\ -1\ \ 0$

Start at -1. Move 2 units to the right. End at 1.   Start at 1. Move 2 units to the left. End at -1.   Start at -1. Move 2 units to the left. End at -3.

The following rules of addition can also be used to add integers.

> **Rules of Addition**
>
> When adding numbers with the *same* sign:
> 1. Add their absolute values.
> 2. Attach the common sign.
>
> When adding numbers with *opposite* signs:
> 1. Subtract the smaller absolute value from the larger absolute value.
> 2. Attach the sign of the number with the larger absolute value.

EXAMPLE 1 ────────────────────────────────

Find the sum.

a. $-1 + (-3)$ $\qquad\qquad\qquad\qquad$ **b.** $5 + (-7)$

(continued)

Algebra 2
 Basic Skills Workbook: Diagnosis and Remediation

Topic 1

Operations with Integers

SOLUTION

a. $-1 + (-3) = -(|-1| + |-3|)$ Add absolute values. Attach the common sign.
$$= -4$$

b. $5 + (-7) = -(|-7| - |5|)$ Subtract the smaller absolute value. Attach the
$$= -2$$ sign of the number with the larger absolute value.

The following addition properties will help you find sums of positive and negative numbers.

Properties of Addition

Commutative Property
The order in which two numbers are added does not change the sum.
   Example: $3 + (-2) = (-2) + 3$

Associative Property
The way you group three numbers when adding does not change the sum.
   Example: $(-5 + 6) + 2 = -5 + (6 + 2)$

Identity Property
The sum of a number and zero is the number.
   Example: $-1 + 0 = -1$

Inverse Property
The sum of a number and its opposite is zero.
   Example: $-5 + 5 = 0$

Find the sum.

1. $-5 + 2$ **2.** $4 + (-7)$ **3.** $-6 + (-4)$ **4.** $-8 + 7$

Subtraction of integers is equivalent to adding the opposite of a number.

EXAMPLE 2

Find the difference.

a. $-4 - 1$ **b.** $-5 - (-7)$

SOLUTION

a. $-4 - 1 = -4 + (-1)$ Add the opposite of 1.
$$= -5$$ Use rules of addition.

b. $-5 - (-7) = -5 + 7$ Add the opposite of -7.
$$= 2$$ Use rules of addition.

(continued)

Operations with Integers

Subtract.

5. $6 - 1$ **6.** $-3 - 2$ **7.** $-5 - (-3)$ **8.** $-7 - 4$

Multiplication of integers can be modeled as repeated addition. For example, $4 \times (-3) = (-3) + (-3) + (-3) + (-3)$. The product of a positive number and a negative number is a negative number, and the product of two negative numbers is a positive number.

The Sign of a Product

- A product is negative if it has an *odd* number of negative factors.
- A product is positive if it has an *even* number of negative factors.

EXAMPLE 3

Find the product.

a. $(-3)(2)(4)$ **b.** $(-3)(2)(-4)$

SOLUTION

a. $(-3)(2)(4) = -24$ One negative factor

b. $(-3)(2)(-4) = 24$ Two negative factors

The following multiplication properties will help you find products of positive and negative numbers.

Properties of Multiplication

Commutative Property
The order in which two numbers are multiplied does not change the sum.
   Example: $4 \cdot (-5) = (-5) \cdot 4$

Associative Property
The way you group three numbers when multiplying does not change the product.
   Example: $(5 \cdot 3) \cdot 4 = 5 \cdot (3 \cdot 4)$

Distributive Property
The product of a number and the sum (or difference) of two numbers is equal to the sum (or difference) of the two products.
   Example: $2 \cdot (4 + 3) = (2 \cdot 4) + (2 \cdot 3)$; $5 \cdot (3 - 1) = (5 \cdot 3) - (5 \cdot 1)$

Identity Property
The product of a number and one is the number.
   Example: $5 \cdot 1 = 5$

Property of Zero
The product of a number and zero is zero.
   Example: $-5 \cdot 0 = 0$

(continued)

Operations with Integers

Multiply.

9. $(-3)(2)$ **10.** $(-3)(-2)$ **11.** $(-3)(-5)(4)$ **12.** $(-3)(-5)(-6)$

Division of integers can be modeled after the multiplication of two integers. For example, $24 \div 4 = 6$ because $6 \cdot 4 = 24$.

The Sign of a Quotient

- The quotient of two numbers with the *same* sign is *positive*.
- The quotient of two numbers with *opposite* signs is *negative*.

EXAMPLE 4

Find the quotient.

a. $-18 \div (-6)$ **b.** $(-15) \div 3$

SOLUTION

a. $\dfrac{-18}{-6} = 3$ Same sign: quotient is positive.

b. $\dfrac{-15}{3} = -5$ Opposite signs: quotient is negative.

Divide.

13. $8 \div 4$ **14.** $(-12) \div (-4)$ **15.** $(-56) \div 7$ **16.** $(72) \div (-8)$

Mathematicians have established an order of operations to evaluate an expression involving more than one operation. The rules are as follows.

Order of Operations

1. First do operations that occur within grouping symbols (parentheses, brackets, and fraction bars).
2. Next evaluate powers.
3. Then do multiplications and divisions from left to right.
4. Finally, do additions and subtractions from left to right.

EXAMPLE 5

Evaluate the expression.

a. $16 + 4 \div 2 - 3$ **b.** $\dfrac{7 \cdot 4}{8 + 7^2 - 1}$

(continued)

NAME _____ DATE _____

Operations with Integers

SOLUTION

a. $16 + 4 \div 2 - 3 = 16 + (4 \div 2) - 3$ Divide first.

$\qquad\qquad\qquad = 16 + 2 - 3$

$\qquad\qquad\qquad = (16 + 2) - 3$ Work from left to right.

$\qquad\qquad\qquad = 18 - 3$

$\qquad\qquad\qquad = 15$

b. $\dfrac{7 \cdot 4}{8 + 7^2 - 1} = \dfrac{7 \cdot 4}{8 + 49 - 1}$ Evaluate power.

$\qquad\qquad = \dfrac{28}{8 + 49 - 1}$ Simplify numerator.

$\qquad\qquad = \dfrac{28}{57 - 1}$ Work from left to right.

$\qquad\qquad = \dfrac{28}{56}$ Subtract.

$\qquad\qquad = \dfrac{1}{2}$ Simplify.

Evaluate the expression.

17. $4 + 9 - 1$ 　　　　　　**18.** $16 \div 8 \cdot 2^2$ 　　　　　　**19.** $6 \div 3 + 2 \cdot 7$

Mixed Review

20. Add $125 + 658$.

21. Compare the two numbers 34.23 and 34.32. Write the answer using
$<, =,$ or $>$.

NAME _____ DATE _____

Quick Check

Review of area and perimeter of polygons

Standardized Testing Quick Check

1. A triangle is 12 centimeters high and its base is 6 centimeters long. Find the area of the triangle.

   A 72 cm²

   B 36 cm²

   C 18 cm²

   D 144 cm²

Homework Review Quick Check

Find the perimeter of the polygon.

2.

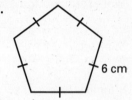
6 cm

3.

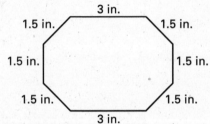

1.5 in.   3 in.   1.5 in.

1.5 in.   1.5 in.

1.5 in.   1.5 in.

3 in.

Find the area of the polygon.

4.

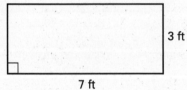
3 ft
7 ft

5.

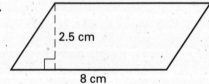
2.5 cm
8 cm

Algebra 2
Basic Skills Workbook: Diagnosis and Remediation

NAME _____ DATE _____

Practice

For use with Lesson 1.1: Operations with Integers

Evaluate the expression.

1. $-4 + 3$

2. $-7 - 18$

3. $4(-3)$

4. $-8 \div (-2)$

5. -24×2

6. $7 - 9$

7. $25 \times (-3) \times 2$

8. $-9 \cdot 0$

9. $40 \div (-8)$

10. $9 \div (-1)$

11. $-36 + 36$

12. $3(2 - 7)$

13. $8 \cdot (-2 \cdot 3)$

14. $(4 + 8) - 7$

15. $-7(-3 + 2)$

16. $84 - 90$

17. $-44 \div (-4)$

18. $-3 \cdot (-2) \cdot (-4) \cdot 5$

19. $32 - 84$

20. $-3(2 + 4)$

21. $62 \div (-2)$

22. $3 \cdot 2 + 16$

23. $5 + 8 \cdot 2 - 4$

24. $10 \div (3 + 2) + 6$

25. $[10 + (5^2 \cdot 2) \div 5]$

26. $\dfrac{20 + 4}{4 + 3^2 - 1}$

27. $\dfrac{18 \div 2}{3(5 - 2)}$

28. $11 - 24(8 - 5) \div 2^2$

29. $6 \div [4 - (6 - 8)] + 3^2$

30. $-3^2 + 4[16 \div (3 - 5)]$

31. $18 \div 2 - 4^2 - (-4)^2$

Identify the property that is illustrated by the given statement.

32. $7 + (-4) = -4 + 7$

33. $7(4 + 2) = (7 \cdot 4) + (7 \cdot 2)$

34. $-6 \cdot (3 \cdot 2) = (-6 \cdot 3) \cdot 2$

35. $8 \cdot 0 = 0$

36. $-3 + 0 = -3$

37. $(-8) \cdot (-5) = (-5) \cdot (-8)$

38. $-3 + (5 + 2) = (-3 + 5) + 2$

39. $-2 + 2 = 0$

40. $-9 + (-7) = -7 + (-9)$

41. $1 \cdot (-32) = -32$

42. *Admission Prices*   The admission prices to an amusement park are $27 for adults, $16 for children, and $18 for senior citizens. There are 6 adults, 13 children and 2 senior citizens in your group. Write an expression to represent the total admission cost for your group. Find the total cost.

43. *Pizza Party*   You and 3 friends buy a pizza for $10 including tax, plus a delivery fee of $2. Write and solve an expression to find C, the cost per person.

Operations with Rational Numbers

GOAL **Add, subtract, multiply and divide rational numbers.**

Terms to Know	Example/Illustration
Rational number number that can be written as the quotient of two integers	$\frac{1}{2}, \frac{5}{3}, \frac{7}{1}, 0.25$
Least common multiple (LCM) the smallest number that is a multiple of two or more given numbers	The LCM of 10 and 6 is 30.
Reciprocal two numbers whose product is 1	$\frac{2}{3}$ and $\frac{3}{2}$ are reciprocals because $\frac{2}{3} \times \frac{3}{2} = 1$.

Understanding the Main Ideas

Before you can add or subtract fractions, the denominators must be the same. If they are not, you must find the least common denominator. Finding the least common multiple will help you understand this process.

EXAMPLE 1

Find the least common multiple of 16 and 36.

SOLUTION

You can find the LCM in two ways.

1. List the multiples of 16 and 36 until a common multiple is found.

     16: 16, 32, 48, 64, 80, 96, 112, 128, 144, . . .

     36: 36, 72, 108, 144, . . .

The LCM is 144.

2. Write the prime factorization of each number.

    $16 = 2 \cdot 2 \cdot 2 \cdot 2$

    $36 = 2 \cdot 2 \cdot 3 \cdot 3$

The least common multiple is the product of the common prime factors and all the other prime factors that are not common. The least common multiple of 16 and 36 is $2 \cdot 2 \cdot 2 \cdot 2 \cdot 3 \cdot 3$, which equals 144.

Find the least common multiple of the pair of numbers.

1. 5, 7   **2.** 9, 15   **3.** 6, 14   **4.** 20, 25

(continued)

Algebra 2
Basic Skills Workbook: Diagnosis and Remediation

NAME _____ DATE _____

Operations with Rational Numbers

To add or subtract two fractions with the same denominator, add or subtract the numerators. To add or subtract fractions with different denominators, write equivalent fractions with a common denominator. When adding or subtracting mixed numbers, you rewrite them as fractions. To add or subtract decimals, line up the decimal points, add zeros as placeholders when needed, and add or subtract as you would whole numbers.

EXAMPLE 2

Add or subtract.

a. $\dfrac{2}{9} + \dfrac{6}{9}$ **b.** $2\dfrac{7}{16} - \dfrac{1}{4}$ **c.** $6.98 + 0.259$

SOLUTION

a. $\dfrac{2}{9} + \dfrac{6}{9} = \dfrac{2+6}{9}$ Add numerators.

$\quad = \dfrac{8}{9}$ Simplify.

b. $2\dfrac{7}{16} - \dfrac{1}{4} = \dfrac{39}{16} - \dfrac{1}{4}$ Rewrite mixed number as a fraction.

$\quad = \dfrac{39}{16} - \dfrac{4}{16}$ The LCD is 16.

$\quad = \dfrac{39-4}{16}$ Subtract numerators.

$\quad = \dfrac{35}{16}$, or $2\dfrac{3}{16}$ Simplify.

c. $\quad 6.98$
   $\underline{+\ 0.259}$ Line up decimals.
   $\quad 7.239$ Add.

Add or subtract.

5. $\dfrac{1}{6} + \dfrac{4}{6}$ **6.** $\dfrac{1}{2} + \dfrac{1}{8}$ **7.** $1\dfrac{3}{7} - \dfrac{1}{2}$ **8.** $6.2 - 3.554$

To multiply two fractions, multiply the numerators and multiply the denominators. To multiply decimals, write the problem vertically. The total number of decimal places in the factors is the number of decimal places in the answer.

EXAMPLE 3

Multiply.

a. $\dfrac{3}{4} \times \dfrac{5}{6}$ **b.** 5.23×6.4

(continued)

Operations with Rational Numbers

SOLUTION

a. $\dfrac{3}{4} \times \dfrac{5}{6} = \dfrac{3 \times 5}{4 \times 6}$　　　Multiply numerators and multiply denominators.

　　　$= \dfrac{15}{24}$　　　Simplify.

　　　$= \dfrac{5}{8}$　　　Simplify fraction to lowest terms.

b.　　5.23　　　　Two decimal places

　　$\underline{\times\ 6.4}$　　　One decimal place

　　2 092

　　$\underline{31\ 38}$

　　33.472　　　　Three decimal places

Multiply.

9. $\dfrac{1}{2} \times \dfrac{3}{4}$　　　　**10.** $1\dfrac{2}{3} \times \dfrac{3}{5}$　　　　**11.** 2.3×6.51　　　　**12.** 3.643×4.951

To find the reciprocal of a number, write the number as a fraction. Then interchange the numerator and the denominator.

EXAMPLE 4 _____

Find the reciprocal of $4\dfrac{2}{5}$.

SOLUTION

$4\dfrac{2}{5} = \dfrac{22}{5}$　　　Write $4\dfrac{2}{5}$ as a fraction.

$\dfrac{22}{5} \longrightarrow \dfrac{5}{22}$　　　Interchange numerator and denominator.

The reciprocal of $4\dfrac{2}{5}$ is $\dfrac{5}{22}$.

Find the reciprocal of each number.

13. 9　　　　**14.** $\dfrac{1}{16}$　　　　**15.** $\dfrac{5}{8}$　　　　**16.** $2\dfrac{5}{6}$

To divide by a fraction, multiply by its reciprocal. The steps for dividing decimals using long division are the same as the steps for division with whole numbers. When you do long division with decimals, line up the decimal places in the quotient with the decimal places in the dividend.

(continued)

Operations with Rational Numbers

EXAMPLE 5

Divide.

a. $\dfrac{3}{5} \div \dfrac{1}{2}$

b. $0.952 \div 0.2$

SOLUTION

a. $\dfrac{3}{5} \div \dfrac{1}{2} = \dfrac{3}{5} \times \dfrac{2}{1}$ The reciprocal of $\dfrac{1}{2}$ is $\dfrac{2}{1}$.

$= \dfrac{3 \times 2}{5 \times 1}$ Multiply numerators and denominators.

$= \dfrac{6}{5}$, or $1\dfrac{1}{5}$ Simplify.

b. Write the problem in long division form.

$$0.2\,)\overline{0.952}$$

Move the decimal points in the divisor and the dividend the same number of places until the divisor is a whole number. Then divide.

$$0.2.\,)\overline{0.9.52} \qquad \begin{array}{r} 4.76 \\ 2\,)\overline{9.52} \end{array}$$

Move decimal point
one place to the right.

So, $0.952 \div 0.2 = 4.76$.

Divide.

17. $\dfrac{7}{8} \div \dfrac{3}{4}$

18. $2\dfrac{1}{4} \div 1\dfrac{1}{3}$

19. $15.3 \div 3$

20. $23.6936 \div 4.231$

Mixed Review

21. Insert grouping symbols in $5 \cdot 4 + 6 \div 2$ so that the value of the expression is 25.

22. *Temperature* The highest recorded temperature in Colorado is 118°F. The highest recorded temperature in Hawaii is 18°F lower than that of Colorado. What is the highest recorded temperature in Hawaii?

Topic 1

NAME _____ DATE _____

Quick Check

Review of Topic 1, Lesson 1

Standardized Testing Quick Check

1. Your credit limit on your credit card is $1000. If you purchased items for a total of $283, how much credit do you have left on your credit card?

   A $717

   B $727

   C $817

   D $827

2. To evaluate the expression $4 \div 2 \times (7 - 3)^2$, you must first

   A divide.

   B do what is in the parentheses.

   C multiply.

   D simplify the exponent.

Homework Review Quick Check

Evaluate the expression.

3. -5×4

4. $36 \div (-9)$

5. $5 - 4 - 2$

6. $\dfrac{2(17 + 2 \cdot 4)}{6^2 - 11}$

7. $4 + 21 \div 3 - 3^2$

8. $(14 \div 7)^2 + 15$

Algebra 2
Basic Skills Workbook: Diagnosis and Remediation

Add or subtract.

1. $\dfrac{5}{12} + \dfrac{3}{12}$ 2. $\dfrac{17}{26} - \dfrac{6}{13}$ 3. $\dfrac{2}{5} - \dfrac{7}{40}$

4. $\dfrac{1}{3} + \dfrac{5}{12}$ 5. $\dfrac{5}{8} + \dfrac{11}{12}$ 6. $9.2 - 8.75$

7. $\dfrac{1}{3} - \dfrac{2}{9}$ 8. $15.85 + 1.005$ 9. $9\dfrac{2}{5} + 3\dfrac{1}{3}$

Find the reciprocal of each number.

10. 15 11. $\dfrac{1}{18}$ 12. $\dfrac{3}{13}$

13. $3\dfrac{2}{7}$ 14. $\dfrac{5}{9}$ 15. $4\dfrac{1}{6}$

Multiply or divide.

16. 8.2×8.2 17. $\dfrac{7}{8} \div \dfrac{2}{21}$ 18. $35.511 \div 5.7$

19. $\dfrac{9}{10} \times \dfrac{5}{3}$ 20. 1.4×6.3 21. $\dfrac{5}{12} \div \dfrac{5}{32}$

22. $7.788 \div 2.2$ 23. $\dfrac{3}{4} \times \dfrac{16}{27}$ 24. $\dfrac{5}{12} \div \dfrac{1}{6}$

Evaluate the expression.

25. $\dfrac{1}{2} \times \dfrac{8}{9} \div \dfrac{1}{36}$ 26. $\dfrac{1}{2} + \dfrac{1}{6} - \dfrac{2}{3}$ 27. $\dfrac{5}{8} - \left(\dfrac{3}{5} - \dfrac{1}{2}\right)$

28. $\dfrac{5}{6} - \dfrac{1}{3} + \dfrac{5}{12}$ 29. $9.88 \times 3.5 - 0.26$ 30. $7(14.77 - 10.5)$

31. ***Fishing*** You went trout fishing. You caught trout with the lengths (in inches) of $8\frac{2}{3}$, $10\frac{1}{2}$, $8\frac{3}{4}$, $9\frac{5}{6}$, $10\frac{1}{3}$, and $9\frac{5}{12}$. Find the average length of the trout you caught.

32. ***Gasoline Prices*** Last week the price of gasoline was $1.25 per gallon. This week the price of gasoline is $1.33 per gallon. What is the change in the price per gallon of gasoline?

Topic 1

Square Root Concepts

GOAL Find and estimate the square roots of numbers.

Terms to Know	Example/Illustration
Perfect Square a number whose square root is an integer or a quotient of integers	$0, \frac{4}{9}, 1, 4, 9$
Square Root a number that when multiplied by itself equals the given number	The square root of 25 is 5 because $5^2 = 25$.
Radical Sign a sign that is used to indicate the positive square root of a number	The symbol $\sqrt{}$ is the radical sign.
Radicand the number or expression inside a radical symbol	In the expression $\sqrt{49}$, 49 is the radicand.
Radical Expression a mathematical expression that contains a radical sign	$\sqrt{72}, \frac{\sqrt{3}}{2}, \sqrt{\frac{4}{5}}, 8\sqrt{7}, \sqrt{0.25}$

Understanding the Main Ideas

The radical symbol $\sqrt{}$ indicates the positive square root of a number. There is also a negative square root of a number indicated by $-\sqrt{}$. Zero has only one square root (zero), and negative numbers have no real square roots, because the square of every real number is either positive or zero.

Meaning	Positive square root	Negative square root	The positive and negative square roots
Symbol	$\sqrt{}$	$-\sqrt{}$	$\pm\sqrt{}$
Example	$\sqrt{9} = 3$	$-\sqrt{9} = -3$	$\pm\sqrt{9} = \pm 3 = 3$ and -3

EXAMPLE 1 _____

Evaluate the expression.

a. $\sqrt{16}$ **b.** $-\sqrt{49}$ **c.** $\sqrt{0}$ **d.** $\pm\sqrt{0.25}$ **e.** $\sqrt{-64}$

(continued)

Square Root Concepts

SOLUTION

a. $\sqrt{16} = 4$ Positive square root

b. $-\sqrt{49} = -7$ Negative square root

c. $\sqrt{0} = 0$ Square root of zero

d. $\pm\sqrt{0.25} = \pm 0.5$ Two square roots

e. $\sqrt{-64}$ (undefined)   No real square root

Evaluate the expression.

1. $\sqrt{4}$ 2. $-\sqrt{25}$ 3. $\pm\sqrt{81}$ 4. $\sqrt{-36}$

5. $-\sqrt{100}$ 6. $\sqrt{144}$ 7. $\sqrt{-4}$ 8. $\pm\sqrt{625}$

In a radical expression, the radical is a grouping symbol. That is, radicals need to be simplified before multiplying, dividing, adding, and subtracting expressions.

EXAMPLE 2 _____

Evaluate the expression.

a. $7\sqrt{81}$ **b.** $2\sqrt{9} + 4\sqrt{36}$

SOLUTION

a. $7\sqrt{81} = 7 \cdot (9)$ $\sqrt{81} = 9$

         $= 63$ Simplify.

b. $2\sqrt{9} + 4\sqrt{36} = 2(3) + 4(6)$ $\sqrt{9} = 3$ and $\sqrt{36} = 6$

               $= 6 + 24$ Simplify.

               $= 30$ Simplify.

Evaluate the expression.

9. $-10\sqrt{49}$ 10. $\pm 8\sqrt{25}$

11. $18\sqrt{16} - \sqrt{100}$ 12. $6\sqrt{121} + 5\sqrt{64}$

If a number is not a perfect square, its square root is irrational. For example, 3 is not a perfect square so, $\sqrt{3}$ is an irrational number. It is possible to estimate the square root of a number that is not a perfect square as shown in Example 3.

(continued)

Topic 1

NAME _____ DATE _____

Square Root Concepts

Topic 1

EXAMPLE 3

Estimate each square root.

a. $\sqrt{31}$ **b.** $\sqrt{128}$

SOLUTION

a. The two perfect squares closest to 31 are 25 and 36. Since $\sqrt{25} = 5$ and $\sqrt{36} = 6$, $\sqrt{31}$ must be between 5 and 6. So, $5 < \sqrt{31} < 6$.

b. The two perfect squares closest to 128 are 121 and 144. Since $\sqrt{121} = 11$ and $\sqrt{144} = 12$, $\sqrt{128}$ must be between 11 and 12. So, $11 < \sqrt{128} < 12$.

Estimate the square root.

13. $\sqrt{6}$ **14.** $\sqrt{24}$ **15.** $\sqrt{155}$ **16.** $\sqrt{200}$

Mixed Review

Evaluate the expression.

17. $-17 + 25 - 34$ **18.** $7.8 + 5.4 - 10.8$

19. $8 - 18 + 4 - (-24)$ **20.** $29.4 - (-8) + 7$

21. $\dfrac{1}{2} + \dfrac{4}{5} - \dfrac{2}{3}$ **22.** $8\dfrac{1}{2} - 5\dfrac{1}{4} - 2\dfrac{7}{8}$

Algebra 2
Basic Skills Workbook: Diagnosis and Remediation

Quick Check

Review of Topic 1, Lesson 2

Standardized Testing Quick Check

1. You rode a go-cart for $\frac{2}{3}$ mile. Your friend rode for $\frac{8}{9}$ mile. How much further did your friend ride than you?

   A $\frac{1}{9}$ mile

   B $\frac{2}{9}$ mile

   C $\frac{1}{3}$ mile

   D $\frac{2}{3}$ mile

Homework Review Quick Check

Evaluate the expression.

2. $1\frac{7}{18} - \frac{4}{9}$

3. $5.2 - 0.228$

4. $\frac{5}{12} \div \frac{1}{3}$

5. *Profit*   A company had a first-quarter profit of $3,587.68, a second-quarter profit of $2,007.25, a third-quarter loss of $963.35, and a fourth-quarter loss of $1,339.76. What was the company's profit or loss for the year?

NAME _____ DATE _____

Practice

For use with Lesson 1.3: Square Root Concepts

Find all square roots of the number or write *no square roots*. Check the results by squaring each root.

1. 1   **2.** 49   **3.** −4

4. −9   **5.** 0   **6.** 100

7. 0.09   **8.** 0.16   **9.** 0.04

Evaluate the expression.

10. $\sqrt{25}$ **11.** $-\sqrt{64}$ **12.** $\pm\sqrt{225}$

13. $-\sqrt{16}$ **14.** $\sqrt{144}$ **15.** $\pm\sqrt{169}$

16. $-5\sqrt{9}$ **17.** $\pm7\sqrt{36}$ **18.** $3\sqrt{49}$

19. $12\sqrt{4} - 6\sqrt{100}$ **20.** $-10\sqrt{81} + 4\sqrt{121}$ **21.** $2\sqrt{225} + \sqrt{400}$

Approximate the square roots.

22. $\sqrt{20}$ **23.** $-\sqrt{3}$ **24.** $\sqrt{7}$

25. $\sqrt{5}$ **26.** $-\sqrt{10}$ **27.** $\sqrt{115}$

28. $\sqrt{288}$ **29.** $\sqrt{75}$ **30.** $-\sqrt{401}$

Geometry Use the Pythagorean theorem ($a^2 + b^2 = c^2$) to find the missing side length of the given right triangle.

31.

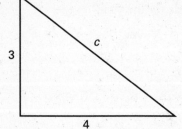

32.

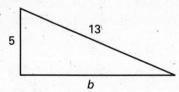

33.

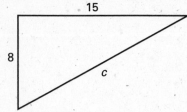

34.

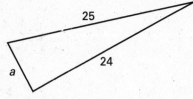

Algebra 2
Basic Skills Workbook: Diagnosis and Remediation

Simplifying Square Roots

GOAL Simplify square roots using the product and quotient properties.

Terms to Know	Example/Illustration
Product Property If $a \geq 0$ and $b \geq 0$, then $\sqrt{a} \cdot \sqrt{b} = \sqrt{ab}$	$\sqrt{2} \cdot \sqrt{8} = \sqrt{2 \cdot 8} = \sqrt{16}$
Quotient Property If $a \geq 0$ and $b > 0$, then $\sqrt{\dfrac{a}{b}} = \dfrac{\sqrt{a}}{\sqrt{b}}$	$\sqrt{\dfrac{4}{9}} = \dfrac{\sqrt{4}}{\sqrt{9}}$

Understanding the Main Ideas

You can simplify a radical expression containing non-perfect squares by using the product and quotient properties. A simplified radical expression is considered completely simplified when there is not a perfect square factor (other than one) in the radicand and there is no radical in the denominator.

EXAMPLE 1 _____

Simplify the radical expression.

a. $\sqrt{72}$ b. $\sqrt{\dfrac{5}{4}}$

SOLUTION

a. $\sqrt{72} = \sqrt{36} \cdot \sqrt{2}$ Use the product property to extract the perfect square.

    $= 6\sqrt{2}$ Simplify.

b. $\sqrt{\dfrac{5}{4}} = \dfrac{\sqrt{5}}{\sqrt{4}}$ Use the quotient property.

    $= \dfrac{\sqrt{5}}{2}$ Simplify.

Simplify.

1. $-\sqrt{48}$ 2. $\sqrt{45} \cdot \sqrt{24}$ 3. $\dfrac{\sqrt{10}}{\sqrt{25}}$ 4. $\sqrt{\dfrac{15}{16}}$

EXAMPLE 2 _____

Simplify the expression.

a. $\dfrac{5\sqrt{3}}{\sqrt{75}}$ b. $-3\sqrt{12}\left(1 - \sqrt{3}\right)$

(continued)

Topic 1

Simplifying Square Roots

SOLUTION

a. $\dfrac{5\sqrt{3}}{\sqrt{75}} = \dfrac{5\sqrt{3}}{\sqrt{25}\cdot\sqrt{3}}$ Use the product property.

$= \dfrac{5\sqrt{3}}{5\sqrt{3}}$ Simplify.

$= 1$ Simplify.

b. $-3\sqrt{12}\left(1-\sqrt{3}\right) = -3\sqrt{12}+3\sqrt{12}\cdot\sqrt{3}$ Use the distributive property.

$= -3\sqrt{4\cdot 3}+3\sqrt{36}$ Use the product property.

$= -3\sqrt{4}\sqrt{3}+3\sqrt{36}$ Use the product property.

$= -6\sqrt{3}+18$ Simplify.

Simplify.

5. $\dfrac{6\sqrt{5}}{\sqrt{125}}$ 6. $\dfrac{1}{3}\sqrt{72}$ 7. $\sqrt{2}\left(\sqrt{27}+2\sqrt{12}\right)$ 8. $\sqrt{81}+5\sqrt{48}$

If a square root appears in the denominator of a number and this number is not a perfect square, such as

$$\dfrac{5}{\sqrt{2}},$$

the square root can be eliminated by multiplying the numerator and the denominator by the radical in the denominator. This process is called *rationalizing the denominator.*

EXAMPLE 3 _____

Simplify the expression $\dfrac{\sqrt{2}}{\sqrt{3}}$.

SOLUTION

$\dfrac{\sqrt{2}}{\sqrt{3}} = \dfrac{\sqrt{2}\cdot\sqrt{3}}{\sqrt{3}\cdot\sqrt{3}}$ Multiply numerator and denominator by $\sqrt{3}$.

$= \dfrac{\sqrt{6}}{\sqrt{9}}$ Use the product property.

$= \dfrac{\sqrt{6}}{3}$ Simplify.

Simplify the expression.

9. $\dfrac{\sqrt{3}}{\sqrt{7}}$ 10. $\dfrac{2\sqrt{6}}{\sqrt{10}}$ 11. $\dfrac{\sqrt{14}}{4\sqrt{2}}$ 12. $-\dfrac{\sqrt{8}}{5\sqrt{3}}$

(continued)

Topic 1

NAME _____ DATE _____

Simplifying Square Roots

In order to add and subtract radicals, the radicands need to be the same. Sometimes it may be necessary to simplify a radical first so that the radicands become alike, as shown in part (b) of Example 4 below.

EXAMPLE 4

Add or subtract the radical expression to simplify.

a. $6\sqrt{2} + 2\sqrt{2}$ **b.** $6\sqrt{8} - 3\sqrt{2}$

SOLUTION

a. $6\sqrt{2} + 2\sqrt{2} = (6 + 2)\sqrt{2}$ Use the distributive property.

$\qquad\qquad = 8\sqrt{2}$ Simplify.

b. $6\sqrt{8} - 3\sqrt{2} = 6\sqrt{4} \cdot \sqrt{2} - 3\sqrt{2}$ Simplify $6\sqrt{8}$.

$\qquad\qquad = 6 \cdot 2\sqrt{2} - 3\sqrt{2}$ Simplify.

$\qquad\qquad = 12\sqrt{2} - 3\sqrt{2}$ Simplify.

$\qquad\qquad = (12 - 3)\sqrt{2}$ Use the distributive property.

$\qquad\qquad = 9\sqrt{2}$ Simplify.

Simplify the expression.

13. $\sqrt{18} + \sqrt{2}$ **14.** $4\sqrt{24} - 2\sqrt{6}$

15. $4\sqrt{20} - \sqrt{45}$ **16.** $7\sqrt{75} + 4\sqrt{27}$

Mixed Review

Evaluate the expression.

17. $-25 + (-16)$ **18.** $75 - 39$ **19.** $(-5)(-14)(2)$

20. $105 \div (-15)$ **21.** $4 \cdot (15 - 8) + (4 - 5)^2$ **22.** $\dfrac{4}{7} - \dfrac{2}{5}$

23. *Recipes*   You want to make $2\frac{1}{2}$ batches of cookies. One batch of cookies requires $2\frac{3}{4}$ cups of flour. How much flour do you need to make all the cookies?

Topic 1

NAME _____ DATE _____

Quick Check

Review of Topic 1, Lesson 3

Standardized Testing Quick Check

1. Which equation is true?

    A $\sqrt{1.21} = 1.1$

    B $\sqrt{6} = 36$

    C $\sqrt{3.6} = 0.6$

    D $\sqrt{100} = 50$

2. Which of the following numbers is *not* a perfect square?

    A 44

    B 121

    C 400

    D 625

Homework Review Quick Check

Evaluate the expression.

3. $\pm\sqrt{64}$ **4.** $\sqrt{100}$ **5.** $-\sqrt{144} + 3\sqrt{4}$

Approximate the square root.

6. $\sqrt{18}$ **7.** $\sqrt{51}$ **8.** $-\sqrt{11}$

NAME _____ DATE _____

Practice

For use with Lesson 1.4: Simplifying Square Roots

Simplify the expression using the product property.

1. $\sqrt{8}$

2. $\sqrt{24}$

3. $\sqrt{45}$

4. $\sqrt{12}$

5. $\sqrt{32}$

6. $3\sqrt{28}$

7. $\dfrac{1}{3}\sqrt{54}$

8. $\sqrt{2} \cdot \sqrt{8}$

9. $\sqrt{7} \cdot 2\sqrt{14}$

10. $\sqrt{2} \cdot \sqrt{5}$

11. $3\sqrt{6} \cdot \sqrt{6}$

12. $2\sqrt{27} \cdot 2\sqrt{5}$

Simplify the expression using the quotient property. Rationalize the denominator when necessary.

13. $\sqrt{\dfrac{1}{9}}$

14. $\sqrt{\dfrac{11}{16}}$

15. $\dfrac{\sqrt{18}}{\sqrt{6}}$

16. $2\sqrt{\dfrac{5}{4}}$

17. $4\sqrt{\dfrac{3}{32}}$

18. $\dfrac{2\sqrt{15}}{\sqrt{12}}$

19. $\sqrt{\dfrac{4}{8}}$

20. $\dfrac{-3\sqrt{2}}{\sqrt{8}}$

21. $-\dfrac{\sqrt{35}}{\sqrt{15}}$

Simplify the expression.

22. $-5\sqrt{3} + 2\sqrt{3}$

23. $\sqrt{45} - \sqrt{125}$

24. $-2\sqrt{2} + 4\sqrt{8}$

25. $5\sqrt{3} - 5\sqrt{2} - 5\sqrt{3}$

26. $3\sqrt{12} - 4\sqrt{27} + \sqrt{75}$

27. $-5\sqrt{8} + 3\sqrt{50}$

28. $2\sqrt{75} - 4\sqrt{3}$

29. $8\sqrt{2} - 3\sqrt{18} - 8\sqrt{2}$

30. $7\sqrt{8} - 4\sqrt{32} - 9\sqrt{50}$

31. $\sqrt{3} \cdot \sqrt{8} + 7\sqrt{6}$

32. **Area** Your square bedroom has an area of 28 square feet. Find the length of one wall.

Geometry Find the radius of the circle with the given area. The area of a circle is $A = \pi r^2$.

33. $A = 44\pi$ in.^{2}

34. $A = 208\pi$ cm^2

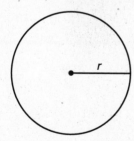

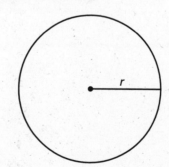

NAME _____ DATE _____

Evaluating Expressions

GOAL **Evaluate algebraic expressions.**

Terms to Know	Example/Illustration
Variable letter used to represent one or more numbers in an algebraic expression	In the expression $7 + x$, x is the variable.
Variable Expression collection of numbers, variables, and operations	$8y, 8 \cdot x, \dfrac{16}{y}, 4 + t, 15 - x$
Evaluating the Expression finding the value of an expression by replacing each variable by a number	Evaluate the expression $2x$ when $x = 2$. $2(2) = 4$

Understanding the Main Ideas

Verbal expressions can be written as variable expressions and then used to solve mathematical problems. Example 1 gives several variable expressions, their meanings, and the operations they indicate.

EXAMPLE 1

Variable Expression			Meaning	Operation
a. $2y$	$2 \cdot y$	$2(y)$	2 times y	Multiplication
b. $\dfrac{12}{x}$	$12 \div x$		12 divided by x	Division
c. $6 + t$			6 plus t	Addition
d. $7 - v$			7 minus v	Subtraction

Name the operation indicated by the expression.

1. $14m$ **2.** $48 \div y$ **3.** $3 - w$ **4.** $x + 22$

Algebraic expressions are useful when discussing quantities where the exact value is unknown. The value of the variables may change or vary with every problem.

(continued)

Topic 2

Evaluating Expressions

EXAMPLE 2

Evaluate each expression when $x = 3$.

a. $6x$　　　　**b.** $\dfrac{15}{x}$　　　　**c.** $x + 7$　　　**d.** $2 - x$

SOLUTION

a. $6x = 6(3)$　　　　Substitute 3 for x.

　　　$= 18$　　　　　Simplify.

b. $\dfrac{15}{x} = \dfrac{15}{3}$　　　　Substitute 3 for x.

　　　$= 5$　　　　　Simplify.

c. $x + 7 = 3 + 7$　　　Substitute 3 for x.

　　　$= 10$　　　　Simplify.

d. $2 - x = 2 - 3$　　　Substitute 3 for x.

　　　$= -1$　　　　Simplify.

Evaluate the expression for the given value of the variable.

5. $11x$ when $x = 6$　　　**6.** $\dfrac{2}{3}y$ when $y = 21$　　　**7.** $\dfrac{7}{9} - t$ when $t = \dfrac{1}{3}$

8. $\dfrac{x - 8}{27}$ when $x = 17$　　　**9.** $\dfrac{36}{x + 3}$ when $x = 9$　　　**10.** $\dfrac{6}{y} - \dfrac{1}{2}$ when $y = 8$

You can use variable expressions to find areas and perimeters of geometric figures as shown in Example 3.

EXAMPLE 3

a. Find the perimeter of the triangle with the given side lengths. The dimensions of the triangle are in feet.

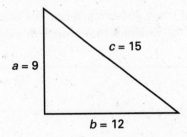

b. Find the area of a square with side lengths of 4 centimeters.

(continued)

NAME _____ DATE _____

Evaluating Expressions

SOLUTION

a. The perimeter of a triangle is equal to the sum of the lengths of its sides: $a + b + c$

$$\text{Perimeter} = a + b + c \qquad \text{Write the expression.}$$
$$= 9 + 12 + 15 \qquad \text{Substitute values.}$$
$$= 36 \qquad \text{Simplify.}$$

The triangle has a perimeter of 36 feet.

b. The area of a square is equal to s^2 where s is the length of one side.

$$\text{Area} = s^2 \qquad \text{Write the expression.}$$
$$= 4^2 \qquad \text{Substitute 4 centimeters for } s.$$
$$= 16 \qquad \text{Simplify.}$$

The square has an area of 16 square centimeters.

Find the given quantity.

11. Area $= \frac{1}{2}bh$

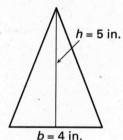

$h = 5$ in.

$b = 4$ in.

12. Perimeter $= 2l + 2w$

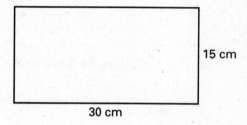

15 cm

30 cm

Mixed Review

Find all square roots of the number or write *no square roots*.

13. 0

14. -9

15. 64

16. 0.36

17. 121

18. -6

19. *True or False?* The absolute value of a number is sometimes negative.

20. *Height* The tallest man that ever lived was recorded to have a height of $107\frac{1}{10}$ inches. The shortest man that ever lived was recorded to have a height of $22\frac{1}{2}$ inches. How much taller was the tallest man than the shortest man?

Topic 2

NAME _____ DATE _____

Quick Check

Review of Topic 1, Lesson 4

Standardized Testing Quick Check

....

1. What is the simplified form of $\dfrac{4\sqrt{125}}{\sqrt{25}}$?

   A. $4\sqrt{5}$

   B. $2\sqrt{5}$

   C. $\dfrac{4\sqrt{5}}{5}$

   D. $20\sqrt{5}$

2. What is the simplified form of $\dfrac{8\sqrt{48}}{\sqrt{2}\cdot\sqrt{8}}$?

   A. $8\sqrt{3}$

   B. $\dfrac{16\sqrt{30}}{5}$

   C. $16\sqrt{3}$

   D. $\dfrac{8\sqrt{6}}{\sqrt{2}}$

Homework Review Quick Check

....

Simplify the expression.

3. $\sqrt{56}$ **4.** $2\sqrt{3}\cdot\sqrt{3}$ **5.** $\sqrt{\dfrac{5}{6}}$

6. $\dfrac{3\sqrt{12}}{\sqrt{8}}$ **7.** $-9\sqrt{6}-12\sqrt{6}$ **8.** $4\sqrt{32}+18\sqrt{2}$

Algebra 2
Basic Skills Workbook: Diagnosis and Remediation

NAME _____ DATE _____

Practice

For use before Lesson 2.1: Evaluating Expressions

Name the operation indicated by the expression.

1. $\dfrac{9}{r}$ **2.** $14 + s$ **3.** $x - 22$ **4.** $30x$

Write a variable expression for the verbal phrase.

5. 15 times x **6.** m plus 27

7. 7 divided by n **8.** 35 minus t

Evaluate the expression for the given value of the variable.

9. $10x$ when $x = 5$ **10.** $b - 16$ when $b = 24$

11. $\dfrac{y}{3}$ when $y = 36$ **12.** $m + 45$ when $m = 58$

Evaluate the expression when $a = -2$, $b = 6$, and $c = -1$.

13. $3(a + b)$ **14.** $\dfrac{b}{ac}$ **15.** $3a - 4b$

16. $25c + 2(b + a)$ **17.** $c - ab$ **18.** $ab(3 - c)$

19. $0.5(3 - a)$ **20.** $\dfrac{1}{2}a + \dfrac{1}{3}b$ **21.** $0.02a + 0.3b - 0.05c$

22. *Perimeter*   The perimeter of a rectangle is equal to $2l + 2w$, where l is the length and w is the width. Find the perimeter of the rectangle at the right. Dimensions are in inches.

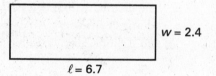

$w = 2.4$

$\ell = 6.7$

23. *Area*   The area of a triangle is equal to $\frac{1}{2}bh$, where b is the length of the base and h is the height. Find the area of the triangle at the right. Dimensions are in centimeters.

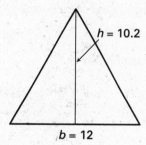

$h = 10.2$

$b = 12$

24. *Average Speed*   The average speed (in miles per hour) is given by the formula

Average speed $= \dfrac{\text{Distance}}{\text{Time}} = \dfrac{d}{t}$. Find the average speed of a car that traveled 180 miles in 3 hours.

Algebra 2
Basic Skills Workbook: Diagnosis and Remediation

Topic 2

NAME _____ DATE _____

Simplifying Expressions

GOAL Simplify polynomials by combining like terms and using the distributive property.

Terms to Know	Example/Illustration
Polynomial algebraic expression with one or more terms of the form ax^n where n is a nonnegative integer (A polynomial is in standard form when the terms are placed in descending order.)	$5x^3 + 2x^2 + 3x + 1$
Coefficient a number multiplied by a variable in a term. (The number is the coefficient of the variable.)	$5x^2 - x$ 5 is the coefficient of x^2.　　-1 is the coefficient of x.
Like Terms terms in an expression that have the same variable raised to the same power	$5x$ and $-3x$; 7 and -2; x^2 and $4x^2$

Understanding the Main Ideas

The distributive property allows you to combine like terms that have variables by adding coefficients. An expression is simplified if it has no symbols of grouping and if all the like terms have been combined.

EXAMPLE 1 _____

Simplify the expression by combining like terms.

a. $4x + 2x + 3$　　　　　　　　　**b.** $6x^2 + 4 - x^2$

SOLUTION

a. $4x + 2x + 3 = (4 + 2)x + 3$　　Use the distributive property.

　　　　　　$= 6x + 3$　　　　　　　Add coefficients.

b. $6x^2 + 4 - x^2 = 6x^2 - x^2 + 4$　　Group like terms.

　　　　　　$= 5x^2 + 4$　　　　　　Combine like terms.

Simplify the expression by combining like terms.

1. $-7 + 4x - 3$　　　　**2.** $5x - 7x + 6x^2 - 8$　　　　**3.** $\frac{2}{3}x - \frac{5}{6}x + \frac{1}{2}$

(continued)

Simplifying Expressions

To add or subtract two polynomials, add or subtract the like terms. You can use a vertical format or a horizontal format.

EXAMPLE 2

Find the sum. Write the answer in standard form.

a. $(5x^3 - 4x^2 + 6x - 3) + (3x^3 + 2x + 4)$

b. $(2x^2 - 2x - 5) + (3x + 4x^2 + 6)$

SOLUTION

a. Vertical format: Write each expression in standard form. Align like terms.

$$\begin{array}{l} 5x^3 - 4x^2 + 6x - 3 \\ \underline{3x^3 \qquad\quad + 2x + 4} \\ 8x^3 - 4x^2 + 8x + 1 \end{array}$$

b. Horizontal format: Add like terms.

$$(2x^2 - 2x - 5) + (3x + 4x^2 + 6) = (2x^2 + 4x^2) + (-2x + 3x) + (-5 + 6)$$
$$= 6x^2 + x + 1$$

Find the sum.

4. $(-2a^2 + 5a - 3) + (15 + 3a)$ **5.** $(8y + 4y^3) + (-7y^2 - 2y)$

6. $(3c^3 + 5c) + (2c^3 - c^2 + c)$ **7.** $(2r^3 + 6r + 12) + (1 - 4r + 3r^3)$

To subtract a polynomial, add its opposite. That is, multiply each term in the subtracted polynomial by -1 and add.

EXAMPLE 3

Find the difference. Write the answer in standard form.

a. $(3x^3 - 2x^2 + 5x - 3) - (-x^3 + 2x - 7)$

b. $(x^2 - 4) - (7x + 8x^2)$

SOLUTION

a. Vertical format: Add the opposite.

$$\begin{array}{r} (3x^3 - 2x^2 + 5x - 3) \\ - \quad (-x^3 + 2x - 7) \end{array} \quad \boxed{\text{Add the opposite.}} \Longrightarrow \quad \begin{array}{r} 3x^3 - 2x^2 + 5x - 3 \\ \underline{+ \ x^3 \qquad\quad - 2x + 7} \\ 4x^3 - 2x^2 + 3x + 4 \end{array}$$

(continued)

Topic 2

Simplifying Expressions

b. Horizontal format: Add the opposite, then add like terms.

$$(x^2 - 4) - (7x + 8x^2) = x^2 - 4 - 7x - 8x^2$$
$$= (x^2 - 8x^2) - 7x - 4$$
$$= -7x^2 - 7x - 4$$

Find the difference.

8. $(4x^2 + 2x - 3) - (x^2 + x + 1)$ **9.** $(-5x^3 + 3x + 2) - (-x^3 + 4x + 2)$

10. $(3x - 7) - (2x^3 + 5x^2 - 1)$ **11.** $(6x + 2) - (-3x^2 + 6x + 7)$

The distributive property can be used to simplify polynomials.

EXAMPLE 4 _____

Simplify the expression.

a. $3(2x^3 + 5x + 1)$ **b.** $4 - 5(2 + x)$

SOLUTION

a. $3(2x^3 + 5x + 1) = (3)(2x^3) + (3)(5x) + (3)(1)$ Distribute the 3.
$$= 6x^3 + 15x + 3$$ Simplify.

b. $4 - 5(2 + x) = 4 + (-5)(2 + x)$ Rewrite as an addition equation.
$$= 4 + [(-5)(2) + (-5)(x)]$$ Distribute the -5.
$$= 4 + (-10) + (-5x)$$ Multiply.
$$= -5x - 6$$ Simplify.

Simplify the expression.

12. $3(x^2 + 4x) + (-4x - 8)$ **13.** $-2(5x^3 - 6x^2 + 3x) - (x^2 - 2x - 3)$

Mixed Review
···

Identify the property that is illustrated by the given statement.

14. $4 + 0 = 4$ **15.** $3(6 + 2) = (3 \cdot 6) + (3 \cdot 2)$

16. $15 \cdot 1 = 15$ **17.** $-5 \cdot (4 \cdot 7) = (-5 \cdot 4) \cdot 7$

18. *School Supplies*   You are buying school supplies at the store. You buy 3 notebooks for $1.29 each, 4 pens for $1.79 each and a backpack for $24.89. How much did you spend at the store on school supplies?

Topic 2

NAME _____ DATE _____

Quick Check

Review of Topic 2, Lesson 1

Standardized Testing Quick Check

1. You drove 220 miles in 3 hours. Which expression represents your average speed if d represents distance and t represents time?

   A. $\dfrac{d}{t}$

   B. dt

   C. $\dfrac{t}{d}$

   D. $d + t$

2. A rectangular computer screen measures 41 centimeters by 31 centimeters. What is the perimeter of the screen?

   A. 1271 cm

   B. 144 cm

   C. 635.2 cm

   D. 72 cm

Homework Review Quick Check

Evaluate the expression when $a = -1$, $b = 2$, and $c = 4$.

3. $6(4ab + 2c)$

4. $\dfrac{2c + a}{b + 5}$

5. $\dfrac{2}{3}(b - a)$

Topic 2

NAME _____ DATE _____

Practice

For use with Lesson 2.2: Simplifying Expressions

Simplify the expression by combining like terms.

1. $17x + (-6x)$ **2.** $-20y + 9y$ **3.** $-11a - 13a$

4. $7 - 2x + 4$ **5.** $-6 - y - 10$ **6.** $5 + x + x$

7. $\frac{2}{3}w + \frac{1}{4}w$ **8.** $2.6p - 3.1p$ **9.** $115x - 140x + 5$

10. $7x^2 - 3x^2 + 4x$ **11.** $30n + 16 - 12n$ **12.** $-2x^3 - 4x^3 + 2$

Find the sum or difference using the vertical or horizontal format.

13. $(5y^2 - 6y + 2) + (4y^2 - 3)$ **14.** $(6x^2 + 6x - 3) - (2x^2 - 2x + 4)$

15. $(3m^3 - 7m + 15) - (4m^2 + 6m - 3)$

16. $(9n^2 - 13) + (-8 + n^2)$ **17.** $\left(\frac{1}{2}x^2 - \frac{2}{3}\right) + \left(-\frac{1}{4}x^2 + 2x\right)$

18. $(-0.5 - 2.2x) - (-6.9x + 8.7)$

Simplify the expression by using the distributive property and combining like terms.

19. $2(x + 4) - 2x$ **20.** $8x - 3(x - 1)$ **21.** $-3(a + 4) + 5a$

22. $-3(x^2 + x - 2)$ **23.** $\frac{1}{2}\left(x - \frac{2}{3}\right) + \frac{2}{3}x$ **24.** $(x - 2)(x + x^2 + 3x^3)$

25. $(2x^2 + 5x - 4x + 7)(-2)$ **26.** $0.04x + 0.75x + 2(0.03x - 1)$

Geometry   **Write an expression modeling the area of the large rectangle as the product of its length and width. Then write another expression modeling this area as the sum of the areas of the two smaller rectangles. Simplify each expression.**

27.

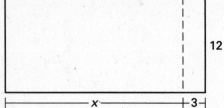

28.

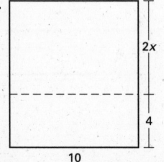

NAME _____ DATE _____

Properties of Powers

GOAL | Use properties of exponents to multiply and divide exponential expressions.

Understanding the Main Ideas

To multiply two powers that have the same base, you add exponents. For example,

$$a^2 \cdot a^4 = \underbrace{a \cdot a}_{2} \cdot \underbrace{a \cdot a \cdot a \cdot a}_{4} = a^{2+4} = a^6.$$

To find a power of a power, you multiply exponents. For example,

$$(a^2)^4 = a^2 \cdot a^2 \cdot a^2 \cdot a^2 = a \cdot a \cdot a \cdot a \cdot a \cdot a \cdot a \cdot a = a^{2 \cdot 4} = a^8.$$

Multiplication Properties of Exponents

Let a and b be numbers and let m and n be positive integers.

Product of Powers Property
To multiply powers having the same base, add the exponents: $a^m \cdot a^n = a^{m+n}$
   Example: $3^3 \cdot 3^7 = 3^{3+7} = 3^{10}$

Power of a Power Property
To find a power of a power, multiply the exponents: $(a^m)^n = a^{mn}$
   Example: $(5^2)^6 = 5^{2 \cdot 6} = 5^{12}$

Power of a Product Property
To find a power of a product, find the power of each factor and multiply: $(ab)^m = a^m b^m$
   Example: $(4 \cdot 6)^3 = 4^3 \cdot 6^3$

EXAMPLE 1

Simplify the expression.

a. $5^7 \cdot 5^3$ **b.** $(t^3)^8$ **c.** $x^2 \cdot x \cdot x^4$ **d.** $[(-2)^2]^5$

SOLUTION

a. $5^7 \cdot 5^3 = 5^{7+3}$ **b.** $(t^3)^8 = t^{3 \cdot 8}$

$\qquad = 5^{10}$ $\qquad = t^{24}$

c. $x^2 \cdot x \cdot x^4 = x^{2+1+4}$ **d.** $[(-2)^2]^5 = (-2)^{2 \cdot 5}$

$\qquad = x^7$ $\qquad = (-2)^{10}$

Simplify the expression.

   1. $x^3 \cdot 2x^5$ **2.** $(z^6)^4$ **3.** $a^3 \cdot a^2 \cdot a^3$ **4.** $(y^3)^2$

(continued)

Properties of Powers

To find the power of a product of factors, take the power of each factor and multiply.

EXAMPLE 2

Simplify the expression.

a. $(4 \cdot 5)^2$

b. $(-3xy)^2$

SOLUTION

a. $(4 \cdot 5)^2 = 4^2 \cdot 5^2$ Raise each factor to a power.

           $= 16 \cdot 25$ Evaluate each power.

           $= 400$ Multiply.

b. $(-3xy)^2 = (-3 \cdot x \cdot y)$ Identify factors.

           $= (-3)^2 \cdot x^2 \cdot y^2$ Raise each factor to a power.

           $= 9x^2y^2$ Simplify.

Simplify the expression.

5. $(x^3x^2)^3$ **6.** $(4x^2y^5)^2 \cdot x^3$

7. $(-2x^2y)^4 \cdot (-3x)^3$ **8.** $-(3x)^2 \cdot (7x^4)^2$

Use the following definitions to evaluate powers that have zero and negative exponents.

Zero and Negative Exponents

Let a be a nonzero number and let n be a positive integer.

- A nonzero number to the zero power is 1.
    Example: $7^0 = 1$

- a^{-n} is the reciprocal of a^n.
    Example: $8^{-3} = \dfrac{1}{8^3}$

EXAMPLE 3

a. $4^{-2} = \dfrac{1}{4^2} = \dfrac{1}{16}$ 4^{-2} is the reciprocal of 4^2.

b. $5^{-2} \cdot 5^2 = 5^{-2+2}$ Product of powers

           $= 5^0$ Add.

           $= 1$ a^0 is 1.

(continued)

NAME _____ DATE _____

Properties of Powers

Simplify.

9. 3^{-3} **10.** $(2x)^0$ **11.** $2^{-5} \cdot 2^5$ **12.** $(6xy^3)^{-2}$

To divide powers with the same base, subtract exponents. For example,

$$\frac{3^6}{3^3} = \frac{\cancel{3} \cdot \cancel{3} \cdot \cancel{3} \cdot 3 \cdot 3 \cdot 3}{\cancel{3} \cdot \cancel{3} \cdot \cancel{3}} = 3 \cdot 3 \cdot 3 = 3^{6-3} = 3^3$$

Division Properties of Exponents

Let a and b be numbers and let m and n be positive integers.

Quotient of Powers Property

To divide powers having the same base, subtract the exponents: $\dfrac{a^m}{a^n} = a^{m-n}$

    Example: $\dfrac{3^7}{3^5} = 3^{7-5} = 3^2$

Power of a Quotient Property

To find the power of a quotient, find the power of the numerator and the

power of the denominator and divide: $\left(\dfrac{a}{b}\right)^m = \dfrac{a^m}{b^m}$

    Example: $\left(\dfrac{4}{5}\right)^6 = \dfrac{4^6}{5^6}$

EXAMPLE 4

Simplify the expression.

a. $\dfrac{x^5}{x^3}$ **b.** $\dfrac{(-4)^2}{(-4)^2}$ **c.** $\left(\dfrac{x}{y}\right)^4$ **d.** $\left(\dfrac{2}{3}\right)^{-2}$

SOLUTION

a. $\dfrac{x^5}{x^3} = x^{5-3} = x^2, \ x \neq 0$ **b.** $\dfrac{(-4)^2}{(-4)^2} = (-4)^{2-2} = (-4)^0 = 1$

c. $\left(\dfrac{x}{y}\right)^4 = \dfrac{x^4}{y^4}, \ y \neq 0$ **d.** $\left(\dfrac{2}{3}\right)^{-2} = \dfrac{2^{-2}}{3^{-2}} = \dfrac{3^2}{2^2} = \dfrac{9}{4}$

Use the division properties of powers to simplify.

13. $-\dfrac{x^7}{x^4}$ **14.** $\dfrac{(2x)^2}{(2x)^4}$ **15.** $\left(\dfrac{3x}{5}\right)^{-2}$ **16.** $\dfrac{(-4x)^{-2}}{2x}$

Mixed Review
....

Approximate the square root.

17. $\sqrt{15}$ **18.** $\sqrt{76}$ **19.** $-\sqrt{41}$ **20.** $\sqrt{187}$

Topic 2

Quick Check

Review of Topic 2, Lesson 2

Standardized Testing Quick Check

1. Which expression can be used
   to express the perimeter of the
   rectangle at the right?

   A. $4x - 6$

   B. $2x - 6$

   C. $x(x - 3)$

   D. $2x + 6$

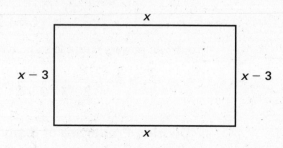

x

$x - 3$ $x - 3$

x

Homework Review Quick Check

Simplify the expression.

2. $3x^2 - 6 + 4x + 3 - 8x$

3. $-9 + 8x + 6x^3 - 2x - x^3$

4. $(2x^4 - x + 6) + (-4x^3 + 2x)$

5. $(5x^3 - 6x^2 + 3x) - (x^2 - 2x - 3)$

Algebra 2
Basic Skills Workbook: Diagnosis and Remediation

NAME _____ DATE _____

Practice

For use with Lesson 2.3: Properties of Powers

Evaluate the expression.

1. $6^2 \cdot 6^5$

2. $(8^2)^3$

3. $(3 \cdot 2)^3$

4. 5^{-2}

5. $\left(\dfrac{1}{3}\right)^{-1}$

6. $12(2^{-2})$

7. $2^{-2} \cdot 2^0$

8. $3^{-9} \cdot 3^9$

9. $15 \cdot 15^{-1}$

10. $\dfrac{4^6}{4^2}$

11. $\dfrac{(-2)^2}{-2^2}$

12. $\left(\dfrac{3}{5}\right)^2$

Simplify the expression. The simplified expression should have no negative exponents.

13. $x \cdot x^7$

14. $(-2y)^3$

15. $(4xy)^2$

16. $(2x^2)^3$

17. $[(-a)^2]^4$

18. $(-x)^2 \cdot (-x)^3 \cdot (x)^4$

19. $[(-2x^5y^2)^2]^3$

20. $\left(-\dfrac{2}{3}x\right)\left(\dfrac{6}{7}x^4\right)$

21. $(x^2yz)^3(xy^2z^2)^2$

22. $(3x \cdot 2x^3)^{-2}$

23. $(17xy)^0 \cdot (3x)^2$

24. $\left(\dfrac{1}{2}xy\right)^{-2}$

25. $(5x)^0 \cdot 5x^0$

26. $(5y)^{-2} \cdot (-2y)^2$

27. $\dfrac{x^7}{x^6}$

28. $\dfrac{3x^2}{5x^{-3}}$

29. $\left(\dfrac{2}{x}\right)^3$

30. $\left(\dfrac{y^2}{y^6}\right)^{-2}$

31. $\left(\dfrac{2x^7y^2}{4xy^4}\right)^3$

32. $\dfrac{a^3 \cdot a^3}{a^2}$

33. $b^5 \cdot \dfrac{1}{b^7}$

34. **Geometry**   The volume of a sphere is given by
$V = \frac{4}{3}\pi r^3$, where r is the radius and π is approximately
3.14. What is the volume of the sphere at the right in
terms of a?

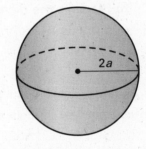

2a

Topic 2

NAME _____ DATE _____

Simplifying Expressions with Powers

GOAL **Multiply and divide expressions with powers.**

Terms to Know	Example/Illustration
Scientific Notation number expressed in the form $c \times 10^n$, where $1 \leq c < 10$ and n is an integer	2.5×10^6, 4.6×10^{-3}

Understanding the Main Ideas

In Lessons 1.1 and 2.2, you learned how to use the distributive property. We can combine this property with the property of powers to multiply polynomials.

EXAMPLE 1 _____

Multiply using the distributive property.

a. $(2x)(5x^2 + 3x + 4)$
b. $(-3x^2)(2x^3 - 5)$

SOLUTION

a. $(2x)(5x^2 + 3x + 4) = (2x)(5x^2) + (2x)(3x) + (2x)(4)$ Distribute the $2x$.
$= 10x^3 + 6x^2 + 8x$ Product of powers

b. $(-3x^2)(2x^3 - 5) = (-3x^2)(2x^3) - (-3x^2)(5)$ Distribute the $-3x^2$.
$= (-6x^5) - (-15x^2)$ Product of powers
$= -6x^5 + 15x^2$ Simplify.

Multiply using the distributive property.

1. $4x^2(3x^3 - 2x^2 + 5x)$
2. $-x(x^4 + 3x - 1)$
3. $-2x^2(x^4 + 1)$
4. $3a^4(-2a^2 + a + 6)$

The procedure for multiplying algebraic fractions is the same as that for multiplying numerical fractions except that you use the properties of powers.

EXAMPLE 2 _____

Multiply.

a. $\dfrac{2x^3}{y^4} \cdot \dfrac{4xy^3}{xy}$
b. $\dfrac{3x^{-2}y}{xy^{-4}} \cdot \dfrac{(2x^3y)^{-2}}{3x^2y}$

(continued)

Topic 2

NAME _____ DATE _____

Simplifying Expressions with Powers

SOLUTION

a. $\dfrac{2x^3}{y^4} \cdot \dfrac{4xy^3}{xy} = \dfrac{(2x^3)(4xy^3)}{(y^4)(xy)}$ Multiply fractions.

$\qquad\qquad = \dfrac{8x^4y^3}{xy^5}$ Product of powers

$\qquad\qquad = 8x^3y^{-2}$ Quotient of powers

$\qquad\qquad = \dfrac{8x^3}{y^2}$ Definition of negative exponents

b. $\dfrac{3x^{-2}y}{xy^{-4}} \cdot \dfrac{(2x^3y)^{-2}}{3x^2y} = \dfrac{(3x^{-2}y)(2x^3y)^{-2}}{(xy^{-4})(3x^2y)}$ Multiply fractions.

$\qquad\qquad = \dfrac{(3x^{-2}y)(2^{-2}x^{-6}y^{-2})}{(xy^{-4})(3x^2y)}$ Power of a power

$\qquad\qquad = \dfrac{3(2^{-2})x^{-8}y^{-1}}{3x^3y^{-3}}$ Product of powers

$\qquad\qquad = 2^{-2}x^{-11}y^2$ Quotient of powers

$\qquad\qquad = \dfrac{y^2}{4x^{11}}$ Definition of negative exponents

Simplify the product.

5. $\dfrac{3x^2}{y} \cdot \dfrac{y^3}{x^4}$ 6. $\left(-\dfrac{x}{y}\right)^2 \cdot \left(-\dfrac{x}{y}\right)^3$

7. $\left(\dfrac{2x}{y}\right)^{-2} \cdot \left(\dfrac{x}{y}\right)^3$ 8. $-\dfrac{2x^{-3}y}{3x^4} \cdot \dfrac{xy^{-2}}{x^{-3}}$

Very large or very small numbers are often written in scientific notation.

EXAMPLE 3

Rewrite in scientific notation.

a. 44,402   b. 0.0056   c. 3.23   d. 0.0000819

SOLUTION

a. $44{,}402 = 4.4402 \times 10^4$ Move decimal point left 4 places.

b. $0.0056 = 5.6 \times 10^{-3}$ Move decimal point right 3 places.

c. $3.23 = 3.23 \times 10^0$ Move decimal point zero places.

d. $0.0000819 = 8.19 \times 10^{-5}$ Move decimal point right 5 places.

(continued)

Topic 2

NAME _____ DATE _____

Simplifying Expressions with Powers

Rewrite in scientific notation.

9. 2,345,000,000

10. 0.000000000617

To multiply, divide, or find powers of numbers in scientific notation, use the properties of exponents.

EXAMPLE 4

Evaluate the expression. Write the result in scientific notation.

a. $(2.3 \times 10^7)(4.1 \times 10^2)$

b. $(2.4 \times 10^4) \div (9.6 \times 10^{-2})$

c. $(3 \times 10^{-3})^2$

SOLUTION

a. $(2.3 \times 10^7)(4.1 \times 10^2) = (2.3 \cdot 4.1) \times (10^7 \cdot 10^2)$ Associative property of multiplication

$$= 9.43 \times 10^9 \quad \text{Simplify.}$$

b. $\dfrac{2.4 \times 10^4}{9.6 \times 10^{-2}} = \dfrac{2.4}{9.6} \times \dfrac{10^4}{10^{-2}}$ Rewrite as a product.

$$= 0.25 \times 10^6 \quad \text{Simplify.}$$

$$= 2.5 \times 10^5 \quad \text{Write in scientific notation.}$$

c. $(3 \times 10^{-3})^2 = 3^2 \times (10^{-3})^2$ Power of a product

$$= 9 \times 10^{-6} \quad \text{Power of a power}$$

Evaluate the expression. Write the result in scientific notation.

11. $(4.2 \times 10^4)(1.6 \times 10^{-7})$ **12.** $\dfrac{7.5 \times 10^{-8}}{3 \times 10^{25}}$ **13.** $(2 \times 10^{-9})^{-2}$

Mixed Review

14. *Temperature* The temperature of boiling water is 212°F. Use the formula $C = \frac{5}{9}(F - 32)$, where F is the Fahrenheit temperature and C is the Celsius temperature, to find the temperature of boiling water in degrees Celsius.

NAME _____ DATE _____

Quick Check

Review of Topic 2, Lesson 3

Standardized Testing Quick Check

1. What is the simplified form of $(-3m^3n^5)^3$?

    A. $-9m^6n^8$

    B. $-9m^9n^{15}$

    C. $-27m^9n^{15}$

    D. $27m^6n^8$

2. What is the simplified form of $\dfrac{x^5 \cdot x^7}{x^{10}}$?

    A. x^{25}

    B. x^2

    C. x^{45}

    D. $\dfrac{x^{12}}{x^{10}}$

Homework Review Quick Check

Simplify the expression using the properties of exponents.

3. $(4x^2y^3)^3$ **4.** $2x^4 \cdot x^7$ **5.** $\dfrac{x^{-3}}{x^3}$ **6.** $(2x^{-2})^0 \cdot (x^3y^2)^{-4}$

NAME _____ DATE _____

Practice

For use with Lesson 2.4: Simplifying Expressions with Powers

Multiply using the distributive property.

1. $(x)(2x^2 + 3)$

2. $(-2x)(5x^2 - 3x + 1)$

3. $(6x)(2x + 3)$

4. $(-4y)(2y^2 - 6)$

5. $(-3x^4)(5xy^2 + 2x^3 - 7)$

6. $(2xy)(-4xy^2 + x^2y - x^3y)$

7. $(7y)(-6y^3 - 2y)$

8. $(-10a)(-a^2 + 3a - 8)$

9. $(5b^3)(9b^2 - 8b - 2)$

Simplify the product.

10. $\left(\dfrac{2x}{y}\right)^3 \cdot \left(\dfrac{-3x^{-2}}{y}\right)$

11. $\left(\dfrac{0.75x}{0.25y}\right)^{-1} \cdot \left(\dfrac{x^2}{y^3}\right)^{-1}$

12. $\dfrac{4x^3y^3}{2xy} \cdot \dfrac{5xy^2}{2y}$

13. $\dfrac{36a^8b^2}{ab} \cdot \left(\dfrac{6}{ab^2}\right)^{-1}$

14. $\dfrac{16x^3y}{-4xy^3} \cdot -\dfrac{2xy}{-x^{-1}}$

15. $\dfrac{6x^{-2}y^2}{xy^{-3}} \cdot \left(\dfrac{3^{-1}x^2y}{xy^2}\right)$

Rewrite in scientific notation.

16. 0.07

17. 86.3

18. 0.0055

19. 625.308

20. $68,000$

21. $3,452,220$

22. 0.00002004

23. $18,000,000,000$

24. $452,114$

Evaluate the expression. Write the result in scientific notation.

25. $(2 \times 10^5) \cdot (4 \times 10^{-2})$

26. $(6 \times 10^{-3}) \cdot (4 \times 10^{-7})$

27. $(1.2 \times 10^4) \cdot (7 \times 10^{-1})$

28. $(4.2 \times 10^{-5}) \cdot (3.3 \times 10^2)$

29. $\dfrac{6 \times 10^{-2}}{3 \times 10^{-6}}$

30. $\dfrac{1.6 \times 10^{-1}}{3.2 \times 10^{-5}}$

31. $\dfrac{8.1 \times 10^{-2}}{2.7 \times 10^{-2}}$

32. $(5 \times 10^{-2})^2$

33. $(3 \times 10^4)^3$

34. $(2 \times 10^{-5})^{-4}$

35. *Size of Earth*   Earth has a radius of about 3.9×10^3 miles. Use the equation $V = \frac{4}{3}\pi r^3$ to find Earth's volume.

LESSON 3.1

Solving Equations

GOAL Solve linear equations using addition, subtraction, multiplication, and division.

Terms to Know	Example/Illustration
Equivalent equations equations with the same solution(s)	$x + 3 = 5$ and $x = 2$ are equivalent equations because each has the number 2 as its only solution
Inverse operations two operations that undo each other	addition and subtraction, multiplication and division

Understanding the Main Ideas

You can solve an equation by writing an equivalent equation that has the variable alone, or isolated, on one side. To transform an equation into an equivalent equation, think of an equation as having two sides that are in balance. Any transformation that you apply to an equation must keep the equation in balance. The inverse operations help you isolate the variable in an equation. The transformations used to isolate the variable are based on the rules of algebra called the *properties of equality.*

Properties of Equality

Addition Property of Equality If $a = b$, then $a + c = b + c$.

Subtraction Property of Equality If $a = b$, then $a - c = b - c$.

Multiplication Property of Equality If $a = b$, then $ca = cb$.

Division Property of Equality If $a = b$ and $c \neq 0$, then $\dfrac{a}{c} = \dfrac{b}{c}$.

EXAMPLE 1

Solve the equation.

a. $x - 15 = 14$ **b.** $52 = y + 16$

SOLUTION

a.

$x - 15 = 14$	Write original equation.
$x - 15 + 15 = 14 + 15$	Add 15 to each side.
$x = 29$	Solution: x is isolated.

(continued)

Algebra 2
Basic Skills Workbook: Diagnosis and Remediation

Solving Equations

b.	$52 = y + 16$	Write original equation.
	$52 - 16 = y + 16 - 16$	Subtract 16 from each side.
	$36 = y$	Solution: y is isolated.

Solve the equation.

1. $n + 17 = 98$ **2.** $907 = m + 316$ **3.** $x + 3.9 = 1.7$

Multiplying both sides of an equation by the same nonzero number or dividing both sides of an equation by the same nonzero number produces an equivalent equation.

EXAMPLE 2

Solve the equation.

a. $-5x = 25$ **b.** $12 = \dfrac{n}{4}$

SOLUTION

a.	$-5x = 25$	Write original equation.
	$\dfrac{-5x}{-5} = \dfrac{25}{-5}$	Divide each side by -5.
	$x = -5$	Solution: x is isolated.
b.	$12 = \dfrac{n}{4}$	Write original equation.
	$4 \cdot 12 = 4 \cdot \dfrac{n}{4}$	Multiply each side by 4.
	$48 = n$	Solution: n is isolated.

Solve the equation.

4. $12x = -144$ **5.** $\dfrac{x}{3.2} = 18$ **6.** $-4.8y = 36$ **7.** $\dfrac{1}{3}t = 82$

Solving an equation may require two or more transformations. In this case, simplify one or both sides of the equation (if needed) and use inverse operations to isolate the variable.

(continued)

Topic 3

NAME _____ DATE _____

Solving Equations

EXAMPLE 3

Solve the equation.

a. $\frac{1}{3}x + 4 = -8$ **b.** $4x - 8 = 24$

SOLUTION

a. $\frac{1}{3}x + 4 = -8$ Write original equation.

$\frac{1}{3}x + 4 - 4 = -8 - 4$ Subtract 4 from each side.

$\frac{1}{3}x = -12$ Simplify.

$3\left(\frac{1}{3}x\right) = 3(-12)$ Multiply each side by 3.

$x = -36$ Solution: x is isolated.

b. $4x - 8 = 24$ Write original equation.

$4x - 8 + 8 = 24 + 8$ Add 8 to each side.

$4x = 32$ Simplify.

$\frac{4x}{4} = \frac{32}{4}$ Divide each side by 4.

$x = 8$ Solution: x is isolated.

Solve the equation.

8. $2x + 7 = 15$ **9.** $\frac{x}{3} - 5 = -1$ **10.** $30 = 16 + \frac{1}{5}x$

It may be necessary to set up equations to solve problems like finding angle measures in a triangle as shown in Example 4.

EXAMPLE 4

Find the measure of each angle in the triangle below.

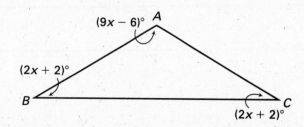

(continued)

NAME _____ DATE _____

Solving Equations

SOLUTION

The sum of the measures of a triangle is equal to 180°.

$m\angle A + m\angle B + m\angle C = 180°$	Write formula.
$(9x - 6)° + (2x + 2)° + (2x + 2)° = 180°$	Substitute.
$(9x + 2x + 2x) + (-6 + 2 + 2) = 180$	Group like terms.
$13x - 2 = 180$	Combine like terms.
$13x - 2 + 2 = 180 + 2$	Add 2 to each side.
$13x = 182$	Simplify.
$\dfrac{13x}{13} = \dfrac{182}{13}$	Divide each side by 13.
$x = 14$	Simplify.

So, $m\angle A = (9(14) - 6)° = 120°$, $m\angle B = (2(14) + 2)° = 30°$, and

$m\angle C = (2(14) + 2)° = 30°$.

Find the angle measures of △*ABC*.

11. $m\angle A = 5x°, m\angle B = (3x + 15)°, m\angle C = (9x - 5)°$

12. $m\angle A = \left(\dfrac{1}{2}x + 3\right)°, m\angle B = \left(\dfrac{1}{3}x + 42\right)°, m\angle C = (2x - 18)°$

Mixed Review

13. Simplify the expression $3x^2 - 8 + 4x + 5 - 7x$.

14. Simplify the expression $(7x^0y^{-3}z^3)^2$.

Topic 3

NAME _____ DATE _____

Quick Check

Review of Topic 2, Lesson 4

Standardized Testing Quick Check

1. Evaluate $\dfrac{(2.3622 \times 10^4)}{(3.81 \times 10^{-3})}$. Write the result in scientific notation.

   A. 6.2×10^6

   B. 0.62×10^6

   C. 6.2×10^8

   D. 6.2×10^{-12}

2. Simplify $\dfrac{4x^2y^2}{4xy} \cdot \dfrac{8xy^3}{4y}$.

   A. $2x^2y^3$

   B. $2x^2y^4$

   C. $4x^2y$

   D. $2xy^3$

Homework Review Quick Check

Simplify.

3. $(3^2)^{-2} \cdot 3^4$

4. $\dfrac{2x^{-1}}{y} \cdot \dfrac{5x^4y^{-3}}{2x}$

5. $(-5x)(2x^3 + 4x - 7)$

6. Write 27,340,000 in scientific notation.

Algebra 2
Basic Skills Workbook: Diagnosis and Remediation

Practice

For use with Lesson 3.1: Solving Equations

State the inverse.

1. Add 12.

2. Subtract 5.

3. Multiply by 15.

4. Divide by 22.

5. Divide by $\frac{1}{2}$.

6. Subtract -2.

7. Add -10.

8. Multiply by $-\frac{3}{5}$.

9. Subtract $\frac{3}{4}$.

Solve the equation.

10. $x + 7 = 12$

11. $y - 8 = 6$

12. $-4 + p = -10$

13. $5 - x = 0$

14. $\frac{3}{5} = b - \frac{1}{5}$

15. $a + 3\frac{2}{3} = 2\frac{1}{6}$

16. $30 = -3x$

17. $8p = -64$

18. $\frac{r}{5} = -6$

19. $\frac{1}{2}x = 35$

20. $-\frac{2}{3}x = -\frac{6}{15}$

21. $\frac{y}{-4} = \frac{1}{4}$

22. $3x + 2 = -14$

23. $4x - 15 = 9$

24. $\frac{a}{6} + 3 = -2$

25. $20 = 16 - \frac{1}{4}b$

26. $\frac{2}{3}c - 7 = 5$

27. $-7x + 4x = 9$

Find the measure of each angle in $\triangle ABC$.

28.

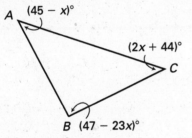

29.

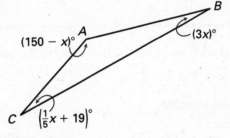

30. *Find the Numbers*   The sum of two numbers is 45. The second number is twice the first number. Find the two numbers.

Topic 3

NAME _____ DATE _____

Solving Inequalities

GOAL Solve linear inequalities using addition, subtraction, multiplication, and division.

Terms to Know	Example/Illustration
Equivalent inequalities inequalities with the same solution(s)	$x - 1 < 4$ and $x < 5$ are equivalent inequalities because they have the same solutions.

Understanding the Main Ideas

Solving a linear inequality in one variable is much like solving a linear equation in one variable. To solve a linear inequality, isolate the variable on one side using transformations that produce equivalent inequalities.

Transformations that produce equivalent inequalities		
	Original inequality	**Equivalent inequality**
• Add the same number to *each* side.	$x - 3 < 5$	$x < 8$
• Subtract the same number from *each* side.	$x + 6 \geq 10$	$x \geq 4$

EXAMPLE 1

Use addition or subtraction to solve the inequality.

a. $x + 8 \geq 5$ **b.** $-4 > y - 8$

SOLUTION

a. $x + 8 \geq 5$ Write original inequality.

   $x + 8 - 8 \geq 5 - 8$ Subtract 8 from each side.

       $x \geq -3$ Simplify.

The solution is all real numbers greater than or equal to -3. Check several numbers that are greater than or equal to -3 in the original inequality.

b. $-4 > y - 8$ Write original inequality.

   $-4 + 8 > y - 8 + 8$ Add 8 to each side.

       $4 > y$ Simplify.

The solution is all real numbers less than 4. Check several numbers that are less than 4 in the original inequality.

(continued)

Topic 3

NAME _____ DATE _____

Solving Inequalities

Solve the inequality.

1. $x + 6 < 8$ **2.** $-5 < 4 + x$ **3.** $8 + x \leq -9$

The operations used to solve linear inequalities are similar to those used to solve linear equations, but there are important differences. When you multiply or divide each side of an inequality by a *negative* number, you must *reverse* the inequality symbol to maintain the true statement. For instance, to reverse $>$, replace it with $<$.

Transformations that produce equivalent inequalities		
	Original inequality	**Equivalent inequality**
• Multiply each side by the same positive number.	$\frac{1}{2}x > 4$	$x > 8$
• Divide each side by the same positive number.	$2x \leq 4$	$x \leq 2$
• Multiply each side by the same *negative* number and *reverse* the inequality symbol.	$-x > 3$	$x < -3$
• Divide each side by the same *negative* number and *reverse* the inequality symbol.	$-4x \geq -16$	$x \leq 4$

EXAMPLE 2

Use multiplication or division to solve the inequality.

a. $\dfrac{n}{5} \leq 11$ **b.** $-4.2m > 6.3$

SOLUTION

a. $\dfrac{n}{5} \leq 11$ Write original inequality.

     $5 \cdot \dfrac{n}{5} \leq 5 \cdot 11$ Multiply each side by 5.

     $n \leq 55$ Simplify.

The solution is all real numbers less than or equal to 55. Check several numbers that are less than or equal to 55 in the original inequality.

(continued)

Algebra 2
Basic Skills Workbook: Diagnosis and Remediation

Topic 3

Solving Inequalities

b. $-4.2m > 6.3$ Write original inequality.

$$\frac{-4.2m}{-4.2} < \frac{6.3}{-4.2}$$ Divide each side by -4.2 and reverse inequality symbol.

$$m < -1.5$$ Simplify.

The solution is all real numbers less than -1.5. Check several numbers that are less than -1.5 in the original inequality.

Solve the inequality.

4. $15p < 60$ **5.** $-10x \geq 100$ **6.** $-\dfrac{n}{5} \leq 17$

Solving an inequality may require two or more transformations. In this case, simplify one or both sides of the inequality (if needed) and use inverse operations to isolate the variable.

EXAMPLE 3
_____

Solve the inequality.

a. $3x - 7 < 8$ **b.** $4 - x > 9$

SOLUTION

a. $3x - 7 < 8$ Write original inequality.

$3x - 7 + 7 < 8 + 7$ Add 7 to each side.

$3x < 15$ Simplify.

$$\frac{3x}{3} < \frac{15}{3}$$ Divide each side by 3.

$x < 5$ Simplify.

The solution is all real numbers less than 5.

b. $4 - x > 9$ Write original inequality.

$4 - 4 - x > 9 - 4$ Subtract 4 from each side.

$-x > 5$ Simplify.

$(-1)(-x) < (-1)5$ Multiply each side by -1 and reverse the inequality symbol.

$x < -5$ Simplify.

The solution is all real numbers less than -5.

Solve the inequality.

7. $15 - x < 7$ **8.** $-5 \leq 6x - 12$ **9.** $7 - 3x \geq 16$

(continued)

NAME _____ DATE _____

Solving Inequalities

Mixed Review

Find the perimeter of the polygon.

10.

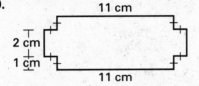

11.

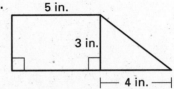

12. A credit card statement shows total charges of $124 and a credit of $150 for a returned item. If the balance last month was $215, what is the new balance for this month?

Topic 3

NAME _____ DATE _____

Quick Check

Review of Topic 3, Lesson 1

Standardized Testing Quick Check

1. Which of these steps can you use to solve the equation $\frac{2}{7}x = 24$?

   I. Multiply by $\frac{2}{7}$.   **II.** Divide by $\frac{7}{2}$.

   III. Divide by $\frac{2}{7}$.   **IV.** Multiply by $\frac{7}{2}$.

   A I only

   B III only

   C I and II

   D III and IV

   E None of the above

Homework Review Quick Check

Solve the equation.

2. $y - 15 = -4$ **3.** $-7 + x = -3$ **4.** $6n = -72$

5. $-\frac{2}{3}t = -70$ **6.** $26 - 9x = -1$ **7.** $\frac{z}{4} + 2 = 0$

(continued)

NAME _____ DATE _____

Practice

For use with Lesson 3.2: Solving Inequalities

Solve the inequality.

1. $x + 8 < 14$ **2.** $-10 < 3 + y$ **3.** $-7 + x > 20$

4. $12 + x \le -8$ **5.** $a - 26 \ge -4$ **6.** $9 \le c + 1$

7. $-5 + b > 0$ **8.** $-2 \le x - 18$ **9.** $n + 7 \ge -10$

10. $13x > 52$ **11.** $-9y < 45$ **12.** $-\dfrac{z}{4} \ge 21$

13. $33 \le -3.3a$ **14.** $-\dfrac{b}{10} > -6$ **15.** $\dfrac{c}{5} \ge -7$

16. $x + 4 < -8$ **17.** $21 - y < 13$ **18.** $-3 \ge 4x + 5$

19. $\dfrac{1}{2}z + 9 \le -7$ **20.** $-19 > -5x + 14$ **21.** $1.2 < -10x - 1.3$

22. $-\dfrac{3}{5}a - 11 \ge 26$ **23.** $8 \le \dfrac{4}{9}y - 12$ **24.** $-3x - 0.4 > 0.8$

Geometry **Write and solve an inequality for the value of x.**

25. Area > 24 square meters

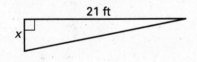

6 m

26. Area < 36 square meters

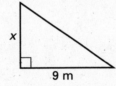

9 m

27. Area $\le$ 42 square feet

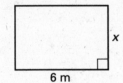

21 ft

28. Area $\ge$ 56 square inches

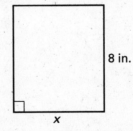

8 in.

29. *Bowling Tournament* After two games of bowling, Carla has a total score of 475. To win the tournament, she needs a total score of 684 or higher. Let x represent the score she needs for her third game to win the tournament. Write and solve an inequality for x. What is the lowest score she can get for her third game and win the tournament?

Topic 3

Solving Multi-Step Equations and Inequalities

GOAL   Solve multi-step equations and inequalities.

Terms to Know	Example/Illustration
Identity equation that is true for all values of the variable	$x + 1 = x + 1$ is an identity because if you subtract x from each side you are left with $1 = 1$, which is always true.

Understanding the Main Ideas

In Lessons 3.1 and 3.2, you learned how to solve one and two step equations and inequalities. In this lesson you will learn how to solve equations and inequalities with variables on both sides of the equation.

EXAMPLE 1

Solve the equation or inequality.

a. $4(1 - x) + 3x = -2(x + 1)$ **b.** $2x - 4 \geq 4x - 1$

SOLUTION

a.
$4(1 - x) + 3x = -2(x + 1)$	Write original equation.
$4 - 4x + 3x = -2x - 2$	Use the distributive property.
$4 - x = -2x - 2$	Combine like terms.
$4 - x + 2x = -2x - 2 + 2x$	Add $2x$ to each side.
$4 + x = -2$	Simplify.
$4 + x - 4 = -2 - 4$	Subtract 4 from each side.
$x = -6$	Simplify.

b.
$2x - 4 \geq 4x - 1$	Write original inequality.
$2x - 4 + 4 \geq 4x - 1 + 4$	Add 4 to each side.
$2x \geq 4x + 3$	Simplify.
$2x - 4x \geq 4x + 3 - 4x$	Subtract $4x$ from each side.
$-2x \geq 3$	Simplify.
$\dfrac{-2x}{-2} \leq \dfrac{3}{-2}$	Divide each side by -2 and reverse the inequality symbol.
$x \leq -\dfrac{3}{2}$	Simplify.

(continued)

NAME _____ DATE _____

Solving Multi-Step Equations and Inequalities

Solve the equation or inequality.

1. $-30x + 1 = 18x$

2. $-7 + 11y = 9 - 5y$

3. $2(6 - a) = -5a - 9$

4. $2x - 1 > 6x + 2$

5. $-5x - 3 \leq 7x + 9$

6. $3x + 2 \geq 7x - 6$

Linear equations do not always have one solution. Some linear equations are identities and some do not have a solution.

EXAMPLE 2

Solve the equation.

a. $3(x + 2) = 3x + 6$ **b.** $x + 1 = x - 3$

SOLUTION

a. $3(x + 2) = 3x + 6$ Write original equation.

$3x + 6 = 3x + 6$ Use distributive property.

$6 = 6$ Subtract $3x$ from each side.

All values of x are solutions, because $6 = 6$ is always true. The original equation is an identity.

b. $x + 1 = x - 3$ Write original equation.

$1 \neq -3$ Subtract x from each side.

The original equation has no solution, because $1 \neq -3$ for any value of x.

Solve the equation if possible.

7. $5x + 24 = 5(x - 5)$ 8. $x - 2x + 3 = 3 - x$ 9. $24 - 6a = 6(4 - a)$

EXAMPLE 3

Solve the equation $3x^2 = 12$.

SOLUTION

$3x^2 = 12$ Write original equation.

$\dfrac{3x^2}{3} = \dfrac{12}{3}$ Divide each side by 3.

$x^2 = 4$ Simplify.

$x = \pm\sqrt{4}$ Take square roots of each side.

$x = \pm 2$ Simplify.

(continued)

Topic 3

Solving Multi-Step Equations and Inequalities

Solve the equation.

10. $2x^2 = 32$ **11.** $\frac{1}{3}x^2 = 27$ **12.** $-5x^2 = -500$

Sometimes you may be asked to solve an absolute-value equation or inequality. To solve an absolute-value equation or inequality, you need to perform two or more steps. You can use the following properties to solve absolute-value equations and inequalities. Study these properties carefully. Notice that it is necessary to reverse the inequality symbol when you are finding the values for which $ax + b$ is negative.

Solving Absolute-Value Equations and Inequalities

Each absolute-value equation or inequality is written as two equations or two inequalities joined by *and* or *or*.

- $|ax + b| < c$ means $ax + b < c$ and $ax + b > -c$.
- $|ax + b| \le c$ means $ax + b \le c$ and $ax + b \ge -c$.
- $|ax + b| = c$ means $ax + b = c$ or $ax + b = -c$.
- $|ax + b| > c$ means $ax + b > c$ or $ax + b < -c$.
- $|ax + b| \ge c$ means $ax + b \ge c$ or $ax + b \le -c$.

EXAMPLE 4

Solve the absolute-value equation or inequality.

a. $|x| = 10$ **b.** $|x| < 6$

SOLUTION

a. ***x* is positive.**   ***x* is negative.**

$|x| = 10$ $|x| = 10$

$x = +10$ $x = -10$

$x = 10$ $x = -10$

The solutions are 10 and -10.

b. ***x* is positive.**   ***x* is negative.**

$|x| < 6$ $|x| < 6$

$x < +6$ $x < -6$

$x < 6$ $x > -6$

The solution is all real numbers greater than -6 *and* less than 6, which can be written as $-6 < x < 6$.

(continued)

Algebra 2
Basic Skills Workbook: Diagnosis and Remediation

NAME _____ DATE _____

Solving Multi-Step Equations and Inequalities

Solve the absolute-value equation or inequality.

13. $|x| = 20$

14. $|x| \geq 17$

15. $|x| \leq 31$

Mixed Review

Evaluate the expression.

16. $-3 - (-7)$

17. $3.6 - 2.4 - (-6.1)$

18. $\dfrac{9}{10} - \dfrac{1}{2} + \left(-\dfrac{1}{5}\right)$

19. $(-6)(-7)$

20. $(3)(-8)(-2)$

21. $16 \div \left(-\dfrac{4}{5}\right)$

Topic 3

NAME _____ DATE _____

Quick Check

Review of Topic 3, Lesson 2

Standardized Testing Quick Check

1. Describe the solution of the inequality $x + 3 \leq 7$.

   A. All real numbers less than 4.

   B. All real numbers less than or equal to 10.

   C. All real numbers less than or equal to 4.

   D. All real numbers less than or equal to -4.

2. At a grocery store, four oranges cost $2.39 and kiwi fruit costs $.69 each. If you have $5 to spend and you buy four oranges, which inequality represents the number of kiwi fruit you can buy?

   A. $x \geq 3$

   B. $x \leq 3$

   C. $x < 7$

   D. $x > 3$

Homework Review Quick Check

Solve the inequality.

3. $0 \leq \dfrac{1}{2}x + 6$ **4.** $\dfrac{3}{4}x + 5 \geq 8$ **5.** $-3x - 7 < 2$

Topic 3

NAME _____ DATE _____

Practice

For use with Lesson 3.3: Solving Multi-Step Equations and Inequalities

Solve the equation if possible.

1. $12x + 21 = 9x$

2. $-2x = 16x - 9$

3. $18x = 9 + 18x$

4. $6 - (-5b) = 5b - 3$

5. $3 - (x - 4) = 7 - x$

6. $20 - 8x = 4x - 4$

7. $3(4 + 4x) = 12x + 12$

8. $-6(3x - 2) = 3(-5x - 1)$

9. $4x - 3 = 15 + 2(7x + 6)$

10. $8c - 4(-5c - 2) = 12c$

11. $8(4x + 7) = 2(6 - 16x)$

12. $\frac{3}{4}(24 - 8a) = 2(5a + 1)$

13. $\frac{1}{2}(12n - 4) = 14 - 10n$

14. $-\frac{2}{3}x = 4\left(\frac{1}{3}x + 1\right)$

15. $-(8n - 2) = 3 + 10(1 - 3n)$

Solve the inequality.

16. $2(x + 1) \geq -2$

17. $\frac{1}{5}y + 12 \leq 8$

18. $-3(x - 5) < 2x - 5$

19. $4x + 1 \leq 2(x + 2)$

20. $-2(-x + 3) > 4(2x - 9)$

21. $-7x - (5x + 2) \geq -5x - 9$

22. $10x + 17 < 4x - 1$

23. $-1 - x > 31 - 6x$

24. $9 + 3x + 1 \leq 3x + 3x + 1$

25. $4(7 + y) > 16 - 2y$

26. $\frac{7}{2}m + 12 \leq 6 + \frac{5}{2}m$

27. $\frac{5}{6}x + 3 > -7\left(\frac{1}{6}x + 3\right)$

Solve the equation if possible.

28. $3x^2 = 48$

29. $-5x^2 = -125$

30. $4y^2 = -16$

31. $\frac{1}{2}n^2 = 18$

32. $-\frac{3}{4}t^2 = -108$

33. $12m^2 = -24$

Solve the absolute-value equation or inequality if possible.

34. $|x| = 14$

35. $|n| = 0$

36. $|m| < -9$

37. $|y| = \frac{3}{4}$

38. $|t| > -\frac{7}{8}$

39. $|r| \leq 1.58$

NAME _____ DATE _____

Writing and Solving Proportions

GOAL **Write and solve proportions.**

Terms to Know	Example/Illustration
Proportion an equation that shows two ratios to be equal	$\frac{3}{4} = \frac{6}{8}$ $3{:}4 = 6{:}8$ $\frac{x}{6} = \frac{4}{12}$
Cross products in a proportion, equal products formed by multiplying the numerator of each ratio by the denominator of the other ratio	The cross products of the proportion $\frac{3}{4} = \frac{6}{8}$ are 3×8 and 4×6.
Solving a proportion for a proportion involving a variable, finding the value of the variable that makes the proportion true	To solve the proportion $\frac{x}{6} = \frac{4}{12}$, use cross products. $x \cdot 12 = 4 \cdot 6$ $12x = 24$ $x = 2$
Similar triangles two triangles that have the same angle measures	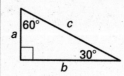 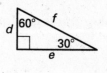

Understanding the Main Ideas

A proportion is an equation that shows that two ratios are equal. Two ratios form a true proportion only if the cross products are equal. In general, the proportion $\frac{a}{b} = \frac{c}{d}$ ($b \neq 0$ and $d \neq 0$) is true only if $ad = bc$.

EXAMPLE 1 _____

Tell whether each proportion is *true* or *false*.

a. $\frac{3}{8} = \frac{9}{24}$
 b. $\frac{5}{9} = \frac{4}{7}$

SOLUTION

a. $\frac{3}{8} = \frac{9}{24}$ Write proportion.   **b.** $\frac{5}{9} = \frac{4}{7}$ Write proportion.

 $3(24) = 9(8)$ Take cross product. $5(7) = 4(9)$ Take cross product.

 $72 = 72$ True proportion $35 \neq 36$ False

(continued)

Algebra 2
Basic Skills Workbook: Diagnosis and Remediation

NAME _____ DATE _____

Writing and Solving Proportions

Tell whether the proportion is *true* or *false*.

1. $\dfrac{4}{6} = \dfrac{6}{9}$

2. $\dfrac{8}{10} = \dfrac{10}{12}$

3. $\dfrac{3}{4.5} = \dfrac{10}{15}$

When one of the terms of a proportion is a variable, cross products can be used to solve the proportion. The cross products are equal, so they form an equation with a variable on one side.

EXAMPLE 2 _____

Solve the proportion $\dfrac{3}{y} = \dfrac{15}{10}$.

SOLUTION

$\dfrac{3}{y} = \dfrac{15}{10}$ Write original proportion.

$3(10) = 15(y)$ Take cross product.

$30 = 15y$ Simplify.

$\dfrac{30}{15} = \dfrac{15y}{15}$ Divide each side by 15.

$2 = y$ Simplify.

Solve the proportion.

4. $\dfrac{10}{40} = \dfrac{7}{x}$

5. $\dfrac{4}{z} = \dfrac{12}{15}$

6. $\dfrac{16}{n} = \dfrac{3}{9}$

Cross products can also be used to solve a proportion that has more than one term with a variable.

EXAMPLE 3 _____

Solve the proportion $\dfrac{5}{2y} = \dfrac{7}{y - 3}$.

SOLUTION

$\dfrac{5}{2y} = \dfrac{7}{y - 3}$ Write original proportion.

$5(y - 3) = 7(2y)$ Take cross product.

$5y - 15 = 14y$ Use the distributive property.

$5y - 15 - 5y = 14y - 5y$ Subtract $5y$ from each side.

$-15 = 9y$ Simplify.

$\dfrac{-15}{9} = \dfrac{9y}{9}$ Divide each side by 9.

$-\dfrac{5}{3} = y$ Simplify.

(continued)

Topic 3

Algebra 2
Basic Skills Workbook: Diagnosis and Remediation

NAME _____ DATE _____

Writing and Solving Proportions

Solve the proportion.

7. $\dfrac{2}{2x+1} = \dfrac{1}{5}$

8. $\dfrac{8}{x+2} = \dfrac{3}{x-1}$

9. $\dfrac{24}{5} = \dfrac{9}{y+2}$

You can write proportions to solve similar triangles. Similar triangles have the same angle measures, but not necessarily the same side lengths. If two triangles are similar, then the ratios of the lengths of their corresponding sides are equal. For the triangles shown in the Terms to Know, you can write

$$\frac{a}{d} = \frac{b}{e} = \frac{c}{f}.$$

EXAMPLE 4

The triangles shown below are similar. Find the value of a.

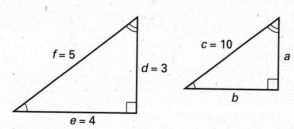

SOLUTION

Begin by writing a proportion that involves a. Then solve the proportion.

$\dfrac{a}{d} = \dfrac{c}{f}$ Ratios of lengths of corresponding sides are equal.

$\dfrac{a}{3} = \dfrac{10}{5}$ Substitute for c, d, and f.

$a(5) = 10(3)$ Take the cross product.

$5a = 30$ Simplify.

$a = 6$ Divide each side by 5 and simplify.

(continued)

Topic 3

NAME _____ DATE _____

Writing and Solving Proportions

10. The triangles below are similar. Find the lengths of the missing sides.

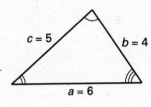 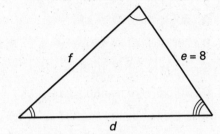

Mixed Review

Simplify the expression.

11. $s(s - s^2)$

12. $3x - 7x$

13. $5 + 4(x - 2)$

14. $8x^2 + 5 - 2x^2$

15. $2x(7 - x) + 3x^2$

16. $\frac{2}{3}x + \left(-\frac{1}{6}\right)x$

Topic 3

NAME _____ DATE _____

Quick Check

Review of Topic 3, Lesson 3

Standardized Testing Quick Check

1. Which equation has the solution -6?

   A. $20(3x + 6) = -246 - x$

   B. $20(3x + 6) = 480 - x$

   C. $20(3x + 6) = 1086 - x$

   D. $20(3x + 6) = 486 - x$

2. Solve the inequality $9x - 4 < 4(3x - 2)$.

   A. $x < \dfrac{4}{3}$ **B.** $x > -\dfrac{4}{3}$ **C.** $x < -\dfrac{4}{3}$ **D.** $x > \dfrac{4}{3}$

Homework Review Quick Check

Solve the equation.

3. $10x + 16 = 2(5x + 8)$ 4. $7y = 3(5y - 8)$ 5. $\dfrac{8}{3}x + 3 = 11 + \dfrac{4}{3}x$

Solve the inequality.

6. $2(x - 7) > 3x + 12$ 7. $-3x - 5 \le -9x + 13$ 8. $\dfrac{1}{3}x - 8 \ge \dfrac{5}{6}x + 2$

Algebra 2
Basic Skills Workbook: Diagnosis and Remediation

Topic 3

NAME _____ DATE _____

Practice

For use with Lesson 3.4: Writing and Solving Proportions

Tell whether the proportion is *True* or *False*.

1. $\dfrac{3}{5} = \dfrac{4}{6}$

2. $\dfrac{25}{3} = \dfrac{100}{12}$

3. $\dfrac{12}{8} = \dfrac{13}{9}$

4. $\dfrac{13}{39} = \dfrac{7}{21}$

5. $\dfrac{0.5}{8} = \dfrac{3}{48}$

6. $\dfrac{12}{2.4} = \dfrac{25}{5}$

Solve the proportion.

7. $\dfrac{x}{9} = \dfrac{12}{15}$

8. $\dfrac{3}{19} = \dfrac{6}{w}$

9. $\dfrac{18}{9} = \dfrac{9}{m}$

10. $\dfrac{4}{2x} = \dfrac{7}{3}$

11. $\dfrac{2}{3} = \dfrac{5}{3c}$

12. $\dfrac{7}{x + 2} = \dfrac{1}{2}$

13. $\dfrac{6}{3} = \dfrac{x + 8}{-1}$

14. $\dfrac{r + 4}{3} = \dfrac{r}{5}$

15. $\dfrac{-5}{6} = \dfrac{w + 4}{2w}$

16. $\dfrac{x + 6}{3} = \dfrac{x - 5}{2}$

17. $\dfrac{x - 2}{4} = \dfrac{x + 10}{10}$

18. $\dfrac{8}{x + 2} = \dfrac{3}{x - 1}$

In Exercises 19–22, pairs of similar triangles are shown. Find the missing lengths of the sides.

19.

$a = 3\frac{1}{2}$ $b = 3\frac{1}{2}$

$c = 2$

d e

$f = 1$

20.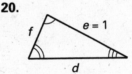

f $e = 1$

d

$c = 1$ $b = 2$

$a = 2\frac{1}{5}$

21.

$b = 4$ c

a

$f = 15$ $c = 12$

$d = 9$

22.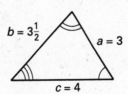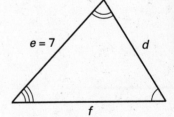

$b = 3\frac{1}{2}$ $a = 3$

$c = 4$

$e = 7$ d

f

23. Bruce traveled 345 miles in his car on 15 gallons of gasoline. How far will he be able to travel with a full tank of 18 gallons?

24. Trisha earned $15.75 in 3 hours at her part-time job. How much would she earn for working 5 hours?

Plotting Points

GOAL **Plot and read points in a coordinate plane.**

Terms to Know	*Example/Illustration*
Coordinate Plane plane formed by two real number lines that intersect at a right angle	
Quadrant one of four parts into which the axes divide a coordinate plane	See illustration above. The point $(2, 1)$ is in Quadrant 1, $(-4, 1)$ is in Quadrant 2, $(-2, -2)$ is in Quadrant 3, and $(2, -3)$ is in Quadrant 4.
Ordered Pair pair of numbers used to identify a point in a coordinate plane	$(4, 6), (-3, 1), (-1, -1), (4, -7), (0, 0)$
x-coordinate the first number in an ordered pair	In the ordered pair $(-4, 3)$, -4 is the x-coordinate.
y-coordinate the second number in an ordered pair	In the ordered pair $(-4, 3)$, 3 is the y-coordinate.
Graph of an equation the set of *all* points (x, y) that are solutions of the equation	

Understanding the Main Ideas

To plot a point in a coordinate plane, you draw the point in the coordinate plane that corresponds to an ordered pair of numbers.

(continued)

Topic 4

NAME _____ DATE _____

Plotting Points

EXAMPLE 1

Plot and label each ordered pair. Determine which quadrant it is in.

a. $(2, 3)$ **b.** $(-1, 4)$ **c.** $(3, -6)$ **d.** $(-2, 0)$

SOLUTION

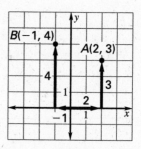

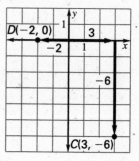

a. To plot the point $(2, 3)$, start at the origin. Move 2 units to the right and 3 units up. From the graph at the right, you can see that the point $(2, 3)$ is in Quadrant 1.

b. To plot the point $(-1, 4)$, start at the origin. Move 1 unit to the left and 4 units up. From the graph at the right, you can see that the point $(-1, 4)$ is in Quadrant 2.

c. To plot the point $(3, -6)$, start at the origin. Move 3 units to the right and 6 units down. From the graph at the right, you can see that the point $(3, -6)$ is in Quadrant 4.

d. To plot the point $(-2, 0)$, start at the origin. Move 2 units to the left and 0 units up or down. From the graph at the right, you can see that the point $(-2, 0)$ is on the *x*-axis. The point does not lie in a quadrant.

Plot and label the ordered pair. Determine which quadrant it is in.

1. $(0, 4)$ **2.** $(-3, -1)$ **3.** $(-4, 5)$ **4.** $(7, 2)$

Give the coordinates of each of the following points.

5. *A*

6. *B*

7. *C*

8. *D*

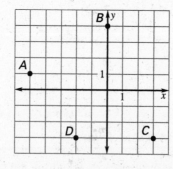

You can use a table of values to graph linear equations. When you make a table of values, choose values of *x* that include negative values, zero, and positive values. This way you can see how the graph behaves to the left and right of the *y*-axis.

(continued)

Algebra 2
Basic Skills Workbook: Diagnosis and Remediation

NAME _____ DATE _____

Plotting Points

EXAMPLE 2 _____

Use a table of values to graph the equation $y - 1 = 2x$.

SOLUTION

Rewrite the equation in function form by solving for y.

$y - 1 = 2x$ Write original equation

$y = 2x + 1$ Add 1 to each side.

Choose a few values for x and make a table of values.

Choose x.	**Substitute to find corresponding y-value.**
-2	$y = 2(-2) + 1 = -3$
-1	$y = 2(-1) + 1 = -1$
0	$y = 2(0) + 1 = 1$
1	$y = 2(1) + 1 = 3$
2	$y = 2(2) + 1 = 5$

With this table of values you have found five solutions.

$(-2, -3), (-1, -1),$

$(0, 1), (1, 3), (2, 5)$

Plot the points and draw a line connecting the points. You can see that the points all lie on a straight line.

The line through the points is the graph of the equation.

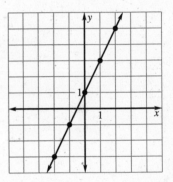

Graph the equation using a table of values.

9. $3x = y + 4$ **10.** $y = -5x + 7$

11. $y + 2x = 10$

Mixed Review

Evaluate the expression for the given value of the variable.

12. $x(5 - 9x)$ when $x = 4$ **13.** $\dfrac{12 - 7a}{a + 2}$ when $a = 2$

Simplify the expression.

14. $4(2x - 9) - 10x$ **15.** $(-6x + 5)(2x) + 15$

Topic 4

NAME _____ DATE _____

Quick Check
Review of Topic 4, Lesson 1

Standardized Testing Quick Check

1. Which of the following is the solution of the proportion $\dfrac{4}{y + 9} = \dfrac{6}{y - 7}$?

    A. -82 **B.** -41 **C.** 41 **D.** 7

Homework Review Quick Check

In Exercises 2 and 3, pairs of similar triangles are shown. Find the missing lengths of the sides.

2.

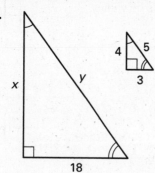

3.

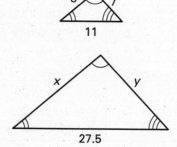

Algebra 2
Basic Skills Workbook: Diagnosis and Remediation

NAME _____ DATE _____

Practice

For use with Lesson 4.1: Plotting Points

Write the ordered pairs that correspond to the points labeled A, B, C, and D in the coordinate plane.

1.
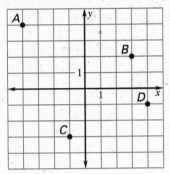

2.
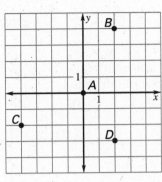

3.
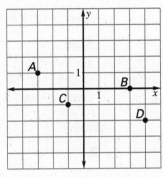

4.
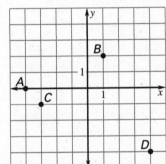

5.
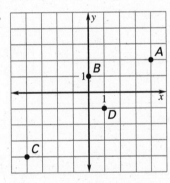

6.
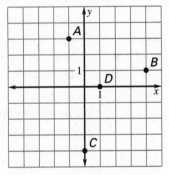

Plot and label the ordered pairs in a coordinate plane.

7. $A(0, 2)$, $B(-1, -3)$, $C(4, 0)$

8. $A(6, 3)$, $B(0, 0)$, $C(-3, -3)$

9. $A(-2, 4)$, $B(0, -5)$, $C(2, 2)$

10. $A(-4, 0)$, $B(-6, -3)$, $C(5, -1)$

11. $A(3, -8)$, $B(10, 7)$, $C(0, 0)$

12. $A(-6, 6)$, $B(1, -3)$, $C(2, -4)$

13. $A(0, 2.5)$, $B(-1.5, -3)$, $C(3, -6.5)$

14. $A\left(\frac{1}{2}, 0\right)$, $B\left(-2\frac{3}{4}, \frac{2}{3}\right)$, $C\left(-1\frac{1}{3}, -4\frac{1}{2}\right)$

15. Plot the triangle with vertices at $A(5, 8)$, $B(-2, 3)$, and $C(3, -4)$ in a coordinate plane.

16. Plot the parallelogram with vertices at $A(-5, 3)$, $B(-2, 9)$, $C(5, 9)$, and $D(2, 3)$ in a coordinate plane.

Without plotting the point, tell whether it is in Quadrant 1, Quadrant 2, Quadrant 3, or Quadrant 4.

17. $(-2, -3)$

18. $(4, 7)$

19. $(-10, 15)$

20. $(-6, -2)$

21. $(9, -8)$

22. $(11, 1)$

23. $(-4, 12)$

24. $(18, -13)$

True or False? Determine whether the statement is *true* or *false*.

25. In the ordered pair $(-6, -8)$, -6 is the x-coordinate.

26. The point $(0, -4)$ is in Quadrant 3.

27. Each point in a coordinate plane corresponds to an ordered pair of real numbers.

NAME _____   DATE _____

Slope-Intercept Form of a Linear Equation

GOAL Graph a linear equation using the slope-intercept form of a line.

Terms to Know   Example/Illustration

Slope number of units a nonvertical line rises or falls for each unit of horizontal change from left or right	The slope m is $m = \dfrac{y_2 - y_1}{x_2 - x_1} = \dfrac{\text{rise}}{\text{run}}$. 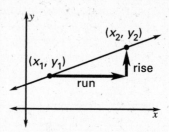
y-intercept the y-coordinate of a point where a graph crosses the y-axis	In a graph, a line crosses the y-axis at the point $(0, 2)$. So, the y-intercept is 2.
Slope-intercept form linear equation written in the form $y = mx + b$, where m is the slope and b is the y-intercept	$y = -2x - 5$, where -2 is the slope and -5 is the y-intercept.

Understanding the Main Ideas

The following example shows how to write equations in slope-intercept form. Once in this form, the slope and y-intercept are easily identified.

EXAMPLE 1

_____

EQUATION	SLOPE-INTERCEPT FORM	SLOPE	y-INTERCEPT
a. $y = -x - 3$	$y = (-1)x - 3$	$m = -1$	$b = -3$
b. $y = \dfrac{x + 3}{4}$	$y = \dfrac{1}{4}x + \dfrac{3}{4}$	$m = \dfrac{1}{4}$	$b = \dfrac{3}{4}$
c. $y = 7$	$y = 0x + 7$	$m = 0$	$b = 7$
d. $3x - 6y = 18$	$y = 0.5x - 3$	$m = 0.5$	$b = -3$

Write the equation in slope-intercept form. Then identify the slope and y-intercept.

1. $y = 3x + 8$ **2.** $y = \dfrac{2x - 5}{4}$ **3.** $y = -1.5$ **4.** $-2x + 8y = 16$

(continued)

Algebra 2
Basic Skills Workbook: Diagnosis and Remediation

Topic 4

Slope-Intercept Form of a Linear Equation

You can graph equations using the slope-intercept form of a line.

EXAMPLE 2

Graph the equation $4x + y = 7$.

SOLUTION

Write the equation in slope-intercept form.

$y = -4x + 7$

Find the slope and y-intercept.

$m = -4 \qquad b = 7$

Draw a slope triangle to locate a second point on the line.

$m = \dfrac{-4}{1} = \dfrac{\text{rise}}{\text{run}}$

Draw a line through the two points.

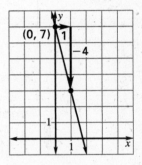

Graph the equation using the slope-intercept form of the line.

5. $y = x + 3$ **6.** $y = 2x - 1$ **7.** $x - y + 6 = 0$

You can write the equation of a line in slope-intercept form given the graph of the equation, as shown in Example 3.

EXAMPLE 3

Write the equation of the line shown in the graph below.

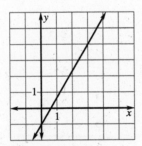

SOLUTION

Find the slope and identify the y-intercept. From the graph you can see that the y-intercept is $b = -1$. The slope is

$m = \dfrac{\text{rise}}{\text{run}} = \dfrac{5}{3}.$

Substitute b and m in the equation $y = mx + b$.

The equation of the line is $y = \dfrac{5}{3}x - 1$.

(continued)

Topic 4

NAME _____ DATE _____

Slope-Intercept Form of a Linear Equation

Write the equation of the line in slope-intercept form.

8. 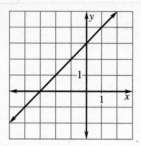 **9.** 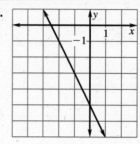 **10.**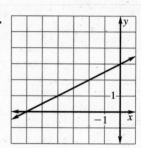

Mixed Review

Simplify the expression.

11. $2\sqrt{2} \cdot 3\sqrt{8}$ **12.** $\sqrt{45}$ **13.** $6\sqrt{12} - 10\sqrt{3}$

Use the Pythagorean theorem to find the missing side length of the given right triangle.

14. 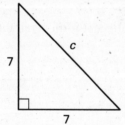   **15.**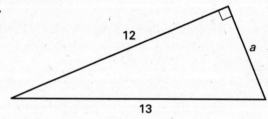

Algebra 2
Basic Skills Workbook: Diagnosis and Remediation

NAME _____ DATE _____

Quick Check

Review of Topic 4, Lesson 1

Standardized Testing Quick Check

1. The point $(-8, 10)$ is in which quadrant?

    A. Quadrant 1   **B.** Quadrant 2   **C.** Quadrant 3   **D.** Quadrant 4

    E. None of the above

2. In the ordered pair $(-2, 2)$, 2 is the

    A. x-coordinate **B.** origin   **C.** y-coordinate **D.** y-axis

3. To plot the point $(4, -9)$, start at the origin.

    Move 4 units ____ and 9 units ____.

    A. right, up   **B.** left, down   **C.** right, down   **D.** left, up

Homework Review Quick Check

Plot and label the ordered pairs in a coordinate plane.

    4. $A(0, 3), B(-5, 5)$ **5.** $A(-2, -6), B(7, 5)$

Write the ordered pairs that correspond to the points labeled A, B, and C in the coordinate plane.

    6. 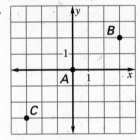   **7.** 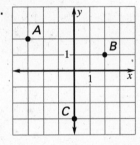

Topic 4

NAME _____ DATE _____

Practice

For use with Lesson 4.2: Slope-Intercept Form of a Linear Equation

Find the slope and *y*-intercept of the graph of the equation.

1. $y = 5x + 1$ **2.** $y = -3x - 1$ **3.** $y = 2x + 7$

4. $y - 3x = 15$ **5.** $y = 4$ **6.** $2x + 4y = 16$

7. $y = \dfrac{1}{5}x + \dfrac{3}{4}$ **8.** $y = \dfrac{x - 2}{6}$ **9.** $y = \dfrac{-3x + 9}{8}$

10. $12x + 4y - 2 = 0$ **11.** $-9x - 3y + 8 = 0$ **12.** $7x - 14y + 2 = 0$

Graph the equation.

13. $y = x + 2$ **14.** $y = 2x - 3$ **15.** $y = x - 5$

16. $y = -x + 4$ **17.** $y = 7 - x$ **18.** $y = 3x + 2$

19. $y = -3$ **20.** $y = \dfrac{1}{2}x - 6$ **21.** $y = -\dfrac{3}{4}x$

Write the equation in slope-intercept form. Then graph the equation.

22. $y = 3$ **23.** $x - y = 1$ **24.** $2x - 4y = 12$

25. $x + y = 0$ **26.** $x + 3y - 3 = 0$ **27.** $4x - y - 3 = 0$

Match the equation with its graph.

A. $y = x + 1$ **B.** $y = -x + 1$ **C.** $y = x + 2$

28. 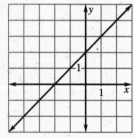   **29.** 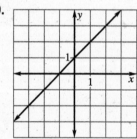   **30.**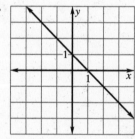

Snowstorm   In Exercises 31 and 32, snow fell at a rate of $\dfrac{2}{3}$ inch per hour. Before the snowstorm began, there were already 5 inches of snow on the ground. The equation $y = \dfrac{2}{3}x + 5$ models the depth y of snow on the ground after x hours.

31. What is the slope of $y = \dfrac{2}{3}x + 5$? What is the *y*-intercept?

32. Graph the amount of snow on the ground during the snowstorm.

NAME _____ DATE _____

Quick Graphs Using Intercepts

GOAL Find the *x*-intercept and the *y*-intercept of a line and use them to graph the equation.

Terms to Know	**Example/Illustration**
x-intercept the *x*-coordinate of a point where a graph crosses the *x*-axis	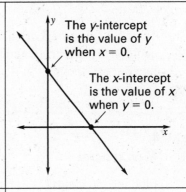 The *y*-intercept is the value of *y* when *x* = 0. The *x*-intercept is the value of *x* when *y* = 0.
y-intercept the *y*-coordinate of a point where a graph crosses the *y*-axis	See the illustration above.

Understanding the Main Ideas

In Lesson 4.1, you learned how to graph a linear equation by making a table of values, plotting the points, and drawing a line through the points. In this lesson, you will learn a quicker way to graph a linear equation. To do this, you only need to find the *x*-intercept and the *y*-intercept. The following example shows how to find the intercepts.

EXAMPLE 1

Find the *x*-intercept and the *y*-intercept of the graph of the equation $5x + 2y = 10$.

SOLUTION

To find the *x*-intercept of $5x + 2y = 10$, let $y = 0$.

$$5x + 2y = 10 \qquad \text{Write original equation.}$$
$$5x + 2(0) = 10 \qquad \text{Substitute 0 for } y.$$
$$x = 2 \qquad \text{Solve for } x.$$

The *x*-intercept is 2. The line crosses the *x*-axis at the point $(2, 0)$.

To find the *y*-intercept of $5x + 2y = 10$, let $x = 0$.

$$5x + 2y = 10 \qquad \text{Write original equation.}$$
$$5(0) + 2y = 10 \qquad \text{Substitute 0 for } x.$$
$$y = 5 \qquad \text{Solve for } y.$$

The *y*-intercept is 5. The line crosses the *y*-axis at the point $(0, 5)$.

(continued)

NAME _____ DATE _____

Quick Graphs Using Intercepts

Find the *x*-intercept and the *y*-intercept of the graph of the equation.

1. $x + y = 5$ **2.** $3x - y = 9$ **3.** $4x - 4y = -16$

4. $2x + 3y = 12$ **5.** $-5x - 2y = 20$ **6.** $x + 3y = 6$

To graph a linear equation using the intercepts, find the intercepts, draw a coordinate plane that includes the intercepts, plot the intercepts, and draw a line through them.

EXAMPLE 2

Graph the equation $4x + 2y = -8$.

SOLUTION

Find the intercepts.

$$4x + 2y = -8 \qquad \text{Write original equation.}$$
$$4x + 2(0) = -8 \qquad \text{Substitute 0 for } y.$$
$$x = \frac{-8}{4} = -2 \qquad \text{The } x\text{-intercept is } -2.$$

$$4x + 2y = -8 \qquad \text{Write original equation.}$$
$$4(0) + 2y = -8 \qquad \text{Substitute 0 for } x.$$
$$y = \frac{-8}{2} = -4 \qquad \text{The } y\text{-intercept is } -4.$$

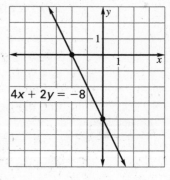

Draw a coordinate plane that includes the points $(-2, 0)$ and $(0, -4)$.

Plot the points $(-2, 0)$ and $(0, -4)$ and draw a line through them.

Find the *x*-intercept and the *y*-intercept of the line. Graph the equation.

7. $x - y = -2$ **8.** $-2x + 6y = 12$ **9.** $3x + 4y = -24$

10. $3x + y = 18$ **11.** $8y = -48$ **12.** $-x + 9y = -54$

Mixed Review

Solve the equation or inequality.

13. $x - 18 < 2$ **14.** $\frac{2}{5}y = -22$ **15.** $-7z \geq -56$

Topic 4

NAME _____ DATE _____

Quick Check

Review of Topic 4, Lesson 2

Standardized Testing Quick Check

1. What is the y-intercept of the line $-4x - \dfrac{1}{2}y = 10$?

   A. -20 **B.** -4 **C.** $-\dfrac{5}{2}$ **D.** 20

2. Write the equation $3x - 4y = 20$ in slope-intercept form.

   A. $y = -\dfrac{3}{4}x - 5$ **B.** $y = 20 - 3x$

   C. $y = \dfrac{3}{4}x + 5$ **D.** $y = \dfrac{3}{4}x - 5$

Homework Review Quick Check

Find the slope and y-intercept of the graph of the equation.

3. $y = 5x - 6$ 4. $y = -10x$ 5. $y + 6x = -7$

Graph the equation.

6. $y = -3x + 2$ 7. $y = 6x - 1$ 8. $2y + 8x = -24$

Algebra 2
Basic Skills Workbook: Diagnosis and Remediation

Topic 4

NAME _____ DATE _____

Practice

For use with Lesson 4.3: Quick Graphs Using Intercepts

Use the graph to find the *x*-intercept and *y*-intercept of the line.

1. 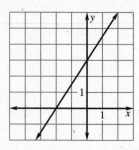   **2.** 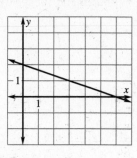   **3.**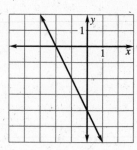

Find the *x*-intercept of the graph of the equation.

4. $x + 2y = 5$ **5.** $-3x + 4y = -12$ **6.** $x - 4y = 8$

7. $5x - y = 20$ **8.** $-2x + 4y = 24$ **9.** $-6x - 15y = 30$

Find the *y*-intercept of the graph of the equation.

10. $y = -x + 3$ **11.** $y = 4x - 2$ **12.** $y - 7x = -15$

13. $-2x + 5y = -40$ **14.** $4x + 8y = 64$ **15.** $2x - 6y = -18$

Graph the line with the given intercepts.

16. *x*-intercept: 3   **17.** *x*-intercept: 4   **18.** *x*-intercept: -7

   y-intercept: -2 *y*-intercept: 6   *y*-intercept: -3

Find the *x*-intercept and the *y*-intercept of the line. Graph the equation. Label the points where the line crosses the axes.

19. $y = x + 4$ **20.** $y = x - 2$ **21.** $y = 3x + 6$

22. $y = -8 + 4x$ **23.** $2x + 5y = 10$ **24.** $-4x + 3y = 12$

25. $x - 7y = 14$ **26.** $5x - y = 15$ **27.** $2x + 9y = -36$

Fundraiser   **In Exercises 28–31, use the following information.**

The girls' softball team is having a spaghetti dinner to raise money for new uniforms. By selling tickets for the dinner, the team hopes to raise $600. Let *x* represent the number of adult tickets they sell at $6 each, and let *y* represent the number of student tickets they sell at $3 each.

28. Graph the linear function $6x + 3y = 600$.

29. What is the *x*-intercept? What does it represent in this situation?

30. What is the *y*-intercept? What does it represent in this situation?

31. What are three possible numbers of adult and student tickets to sell that will make the softball team reach its goal?

LESSON 4.4

Nonlinear Equations

GOAL Graph nonlinear equations using a table of values.

Terms to Know	Example/Illustration
Quadratic function a function written in the form $y = ax^2 + bx + c$, where $a \neq 0$	$y = 3x^2 - 5x + 2$
Parabola the U-shaped graph of a quadratic function	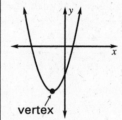
Vertex lowest point of a parabola that opens up and the highest point of a parabola that opens down	See the illustration above.
Absolute value function a function written in the form $y = a\lvert x - b \rvert + c$, where $a \neq 0$ (This function has a V-shaped graph.)	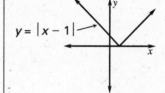$y = \lvert x - 1 \rvert$

Understanding the Main Ideas

You can use a table of values to graph nonlinear equations such as a quadratic equation. To graph quadratic functions, follow the steps described below.

Graphing Quadratic Functions ($y = ax^2 + bx + c$)
Step 1: Find the x-coordinate of the vertex. The vertex has an x-coordinate of $-\dfrac{b}{2a}$.
Step 2: Make a table of values, using x-values to the left and right of the vertex.
Step 3: Plot the points and connect them with a smooth curve to form a parabola.

(continued)

NAME _____ DATE _____

Nonlinear Equations

EXAMPLE 1

Sketch the graph of the quadratic function.

a. $y = x^2 + 2x + 1$ **b.** $y = -2x^2 + 3x - 1$

SOLUTION

a. Find the x-coordinate of the vertex when $a = 1$ and $b = 2$.

$$-\frac{b}{2a} = -\frac{2}{2(1)} = -1$$

Make a table of values, using x-values to the left and right of $x = -1$.

x	-4	-3	-2	-1	0	1	2
y	9	4	1	0	1	4	9

Plot the points. The vertex is $(-1, 0)$. Connect the points to form a parabola that opens up.

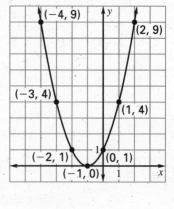

b. Find the x-coordinate of the vertex when $a = -2$ and $b = 3$.

$$-\frac{b}{2a} = -\frac{3}{2(-2)} = \frac{3}{4}$$

Make a table of values, using x-values to the left and right of $x = \frac{3}{4}$.

x	-2	-1	0	$\frac{3}{4}$	1	2	3
y	-15	-6	-1	$\frac{1}{8}$	0	-3	-10

Plot the points. The vertex is $\left(\frac{3}{4}, \frac{1}{8}\right)$. Connect the points to form a parabola that opens down.

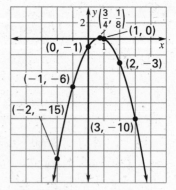

Graph the function.

1. $y = x^2 - 2x - 3$ **2.** $y = -3x^2$ **3.** $y = 5x^2 + 10$

4. $y = -6x^2 + 3x$ **5.** $y = 4x^2 + 4x - 8$ **6.** $y = 2x^2 - x$

You can also graph absolute value equations using a table of values. Follow these steps when graphing an absolute value equation.

(continued)

NAME _____ DATE _____

Nonlinear Equations

Graphing Absolute Value Functions ($y = a\|x - b\| + c$)
Step 1: Find the x-coordinate of the vertex. The vertex is (b, c).
Step 2: Make a table of values, using x-values to the left and right of the vertex.
Step 3: Plot the points and connect them to form a V-shaped graph.

EXAMPLE 2

Sketch the graph of the equation $y = |x - 2|$.

SOLUTION

The x-coordinate of the vertex is 2.

Make a table of values, using x-values to the left and right of $x = 2$.

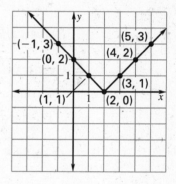

x	-1	0	1	2	3	4	5
y	3	2	1	0	1	2	3

Plot the points. The vertex is $(2, 0)$. Connect the points to form a V-shaped graph.

Sketch a graph of the absolute value function.

7. $y = |2x|$ **8.** $y = -2|x + 3|$ **9.** $y = 3|x - 4| + 1$

Mixed Review

Solve the proportion.

10. $\dfrac{x}{4} = \dfrac{6}{8}$ **11.** $\dfrac{-2}{7x} = \dfrac{4}{14}$ **12.** $\dfrac{x + 1}{20} = \dfrac{2x - 4}{10}$

Find the measure of each angle in the triangle.

13.

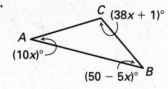

14.

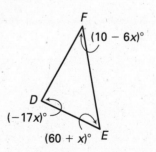

NAME _____ DATE _____

Quick Check

Review of Topic 4, Lesson 3

Standardized Testing Quick Check

1. What is the equation of the line shown at the right?

   A. $9x - 2y = -18$

   B. $-9x + 2y = -18$

   C. $-9x - 2y = 18$

   D. $9x + 2y = 18$

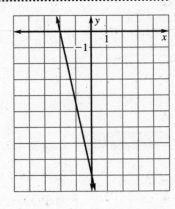

2. What is the x-intercept of $15x - 3y = -90$?

   A. -6 **B.** 0

   C. 15 **D.** 30

Homework Review Quick Check

Graph the line that has the given intercepts.

3. x-intercept: 3

   y-intercept: -1

4. x-intercept: 6

   y-intercept: 6

5. x-intercept: -5

   y-intercept: 4

6. x-intercept: $-\dfrac{1}{2}$

   y-intercept: 3

Algebra 2
Basic Skills Workbook: Diagnosis and Remediation

Topic 4

Find the coordinates of the vertex of the graph.

1. $y = 5x^2$

2. $y = \frac{1}{2}x^2$

3. $y = -3x^2 + 6$

4. $y = 2x^2 + 4x$

5. $y = 6x^2 + 2x + 4$

6. $y = -4x^2 - 4x + 8$

Sketch the graph of the function. Label the vertex.

7. $y = x^2$

8. $y = -4x^2$

9. $y = x^2 + 4x - 1$

10. $y = -2x^2 + 4x - 6$

11. $y = 3x^2 + 2x$

12. $y = x^2 - x - 3$

13. $y = x^2 + x + \frac{1}{9}$

14. $y = 3x^2 - 2x - 1$

15. $y = -5x^2 + 5x + 7$

16. $y = 3x^2 - 3x + 4$

17. $y = -2x^2 + 6x - 5$

18. $y = -x^2 + 4x - 12$

19. $y = -\frac{1}{3}x^2 + 2x - 3$

20. $y = -\frac{1}{2}x^2 - 4x + 6$

21. $y = -\frac{1}{4}x^2 - x - 1$

Sketch the graph of the function.

22. $y = |x|$

23. $y = |x + 4|$

24. $y = |x - 5|$

25. $y = 2|2x - 1|$

26. $y = 3|3x + 2| - 1$

27. $y = -|x + 6|$

28. $y = \frac{1}{2}|4x|$

29. $y = |5x + 5| - 8$

30. $y = |-2x + 20| - 5$

Basketball **In Exercises 31 and 32, use the following information.**

You throw a basketball whose path can be modeled by $y = -16x^2 + 15x + 6$, where x represents time (in seconds) and y represents the height of the basketball (in feet).

31. What is the maximum height that the basketball reaches?

32. In how many seconds will the basketball hit the ground if no one catches it?

NAME _____ DATE _____

Common Monomial Factors

GOAL Evaluate expressions.

Terms to Know	Example/Illustration
Monomial polynomial with only one term	$6, -2x, 15x^2$
Greatest common factor (GCF) the largest number that is a factor of two natural numbers	The GCF of 90 and 84 is 12.

Understanding the Main Ideas

In this lesson, you will factor common monomial factors out of a polynomial. You can use the distributive property to factor out common variable factors. To save steps, you should factor out the greatest common factor. Example 1 shows how to find the greatest common factor of two variable expressions.

EXAMPLE 1

Find the greatest common factor of $14x^2$ and $49x^7$.

SOLUTION

The greatest common factor is the product of all the common factors. Factor each expression and circle the factors found in both expressions.

$$14x^2 = 2 \cdot ⑦ \cdot ⓧ \cdot ⓧ$$
$$49x^7 = ⑦ \cdot 7 \cdot ⓧ \cdot ⓧ \cdot x \cdot x \cdot x \cdot x \cdot x$$
$$\text{GCF} = 7 \cdot x \cdot x = 7x^2$$

The greatest common factor of $14x^2$ and $49x^7$ is $7x^2$.

Find the GCF.

1. $3x, 30x^4$ **2.** $12x^3, 40x^2$ **3.** $58x^6, 14x^4$

Example 2 shows how to use the greatest common factor to factor a common monomial factor out of a polynomial.

(continued)

NAME _____ DATE _____

Common Monomial Factors

EXAMPLE 2

Factor $6x^6 - 15x^4$.

SOLUTION

First find the greatest common factor. Remember that the GCF is the product of all the common factors.

$$6x^6 = 2 \cdot ③ \cdot ⓧ \cdot ⓧ \cdot ⓧ \cdot ⓧ \cdot x \cdot x$$

$$15x^4 = ③ \cdot 5 \cdot ⓧ \cdot ⓧ \cdot ⓧ \cdot ⓧ$$

$$\text{GCF} = 3 \cdot x \cdot x \cdot x \cdot x = 3x^4$$

Then use the distributive property to factor the greatest common factor out of the polynomial.

$$6x^6 - 15x^4 = 3x^4(2x^2 - 5)$$

Factor.

4. $4x^5 + 14x^3$ **5.** $16x^3 - 24x$ **6.** $-22x - 18x^3$

Sometimes you may have to simplify an expression before you can factor out any common factors.

EXAMPLE 3

Factor $3x^2(2x + 4) + 6x(3x)$.

SOLUTION

First simplify the expression.

$$3x^2 (2x + 4) + 6x (3x) = 6x^3 + 12x^2 + 18x^2 \quad \text{Use distributive property.}$$

$$= 6x^3 + 30x^2 \quad \text{Combine like terms.}$$

Then find the greatest common factor.

$$6x^3 = ② \cdot ③ \cdot ⓧ \cdot ⓧ \cdot x$$

$$30x^2 = ② \cdot ③ \cdot 5 \cdot ⓧ \cdot ⓧ$$

$$\text{GCF} = 2 \cdot 3 \cdot x \cdot x = 6x^2$$

Then use the distributive property to factor the greatest common factor out of the polynomial.

$$6x^3 + 30x^2 = 6x^2(x + 5)$$

(continued)

NAME _____ DATE _____

Common Monomial Factors

Factor.

7. $2x(9 - 5x) + 6x$ **8.** $-3x(-4x + 1) - 6x^2$

Mixed Review

9. You have received $700 from your grandmother. If you put the money into a savings account for two years, you will have $700(1 + 0.06)^2$ dollars. How much money will you have after two years?

NAME _____ DATE _____

Quick Check

Review of Topic 5, Lesson 1

Standardized Testing Quick Check

1. What is the *x*-coordinate of the vertex for the graph of the equation
   $y = -\frac{1}{2}x^2 - x + 8$?

   A. -2

   B. -1

   C. $-\frac{1}{2}$

   D. $\frac{1}{2}$

Homework Review Quick Check

Sketch the graph of the function.

2. $y = |x - 1|$

3. $y = -x^2$

4. $y = -|x + 2|$

5. $y = -2|x - 6|$

6. $y = -x^2 + 5x - 6$

7. $y = x^2 + 7x + 6$

Practice

For use with Lesson 5.1: Common Monomial Factors

Find the greatest common factor.

1. 6, 18
2. 32, 40
3. 35, 150
4. $5x^2, 20x$
5. $21x^4, 14x^2$
6. $12x^3y, 18x^2y^2$
7. $42xy^4, 56x^4y$
8. $27x^2y^5, 15xy$
9. $17x^3y^2, 51y^3$

Find the greatest common factor and factor it out of the expression.

10. $24x^3 + 18x^2$
11. $5x^3 - 20x$
12. $6x^2 + 3x^4$
13. $24x^2 - 42x^6$
14. $-3x^4 + 21x^3$
15. $6x^3 - 18x$
16. $4x^4 + 12x$
17. $3x - 9x^2$
18. $25x^5 - 6x^3$
19. $4x^5 + 8x^3 - 2x^2$
20. $18x^6 - 6x^2 + 3x$
21. $6x^4 + 14x^3 - 10x^2$
22. $-3x^5 + 15x^4 - 27x^3$
23. $35x^2 - 20x^4 + 5x^5 + 5x^3$

Simplify the expression and then factor the greatest common factor out of the expression.

24. $3x^4 - 3x(3x^2)$
25. $-(2x)^2 + 14x$
26. $(3x)(5x^3) - 9(3x^2)$
27. $2(5x^2) - 3x(x^4)$
28. $5x(1 - x^2) - 3x^3$
29. $2x^3(6x + x^2) + 4x^4$
30. $-3x(8 - 2x^2) + 4x(3x^2)$
31. $4y(4x) + 6x(4y + 8)$

NAME _____ DATE _____

Factoring $x^2 + bx + c$

GOAL Factor a quadratic expression of the form $x^2 + bx + c$.

Terms to Know	Example/Illustration
Factor a quadratic expression to write a quadratic expression as the product of two linear expressions	$x^2 + 3x + 2 = (x + 1)(x + 2)$

Understanding the Main Ideas

In this lesson, you will learn how to factor quadratic trinomials that have a leading coefficient of 1. To factor a polynomial of this form, you may find a geometric model helpful.

Draw a rectangle and divide the width and length into two parts: x and m for the width; x and n for the length. Divide the rectangle into four regions and find the area of each region. You can see that m and n must be factors of c and that the sum of m and n must be equal to b.

	x	n
x	x^2	nx
m	mx	mn

$$(x + m)(x + n) = x^2 + \underbrace{nx + mx}_{bx} + \underbrace{mn}_{c}$$
$$= x^2 + bx + c$$

EXAMPLE 1

Factor $x^2 + 5x + 6$.

SOLUTION

You want $mx + nx = 5x$ and $mn = 6$. The integral factors of 6 are 1 and 6, -1 and -6, 2 and 3, and -2 and -3. Because $2x + 3x = 5x$, $m = 2$ and $n = 3$.

	x	3
x	x^2	$3x$
2	$2x$	6

$x^2 + 5x + 6 = (x + 2)(x + 3)$

Factor.

1. $x^2 + 4x + 4$ **2.** $x^2 + 8x + 15$ **3.** $x^2 + 9x + 8$

You do not have to use a geometric model to factor polynomials of the form $x^2 + bx + c$. You can list the factors of c and find the pair of factors that has a sum equal to b. In the next example, notice that b is negative and c is positive.

(continued)

Factoring $x^2 + bx + c$

EXAMPLE 2

Factor $x^2 - 7x + 12$.

SOLUTION

You want $x^2 - 7x + 12 = (x + m)(x + n)$ where $mn = 12$ and $m + n = -7$.

Factors of 12	1, 12	2, 6	3, 4	−1, −12	−2, −6	−3, −4
Sum of factors $(m + n)$	13	8	7	−13	−8	−7

The table shows that the values of m and n you want are $m = -3$ and $n = -4$.
So, $x^2 - 7x + 12 = (x - 3)(x - 4)$.

Factor.

4. $x^2 - 12x + 35$ **5.** $x^2 - 9x + 18$ **6.** $x^2 - 10x + 25$

In Example 3, the same method is used as in Example 2, but notice that both b and c are negative.

EXAMPLE 3

Factor $x^2 - 3x - 18$.

SOLUTION

You want $x^2 - 3x - 18 = (x + m)(x + n)$ where $mn = -18$ and $m + n = -3$.

Factors of −18	−1, 18	1, −18	−2, 9	2, −9	−3, 6	3, −6
Sum of factors $(m + n)$	17	−17	7	−7	3	−3

The table shows that the values of m and n you want are $m = 3$ and $n = -6$.
So, $x^2 - 3x - 18 = (x + 3)(x - 6)$.

Factor.

7. $x^2 - 6x - 7$ **8.** $x^2 - 5x - 24$ **9.** $x^2 - 3x - 54$

In Example 4, b is positive and c is negative.

EXAMPLE 4

Factor $x^2 + x - 20$.

SOLUTION

You want $x^2 + x - 20 = (x + m)(x + n)$ where $mn = -20$ and $m + n = 1$.

(continued)

NAME _____ DATE _____

Factoring $x^2 + bx + c$

Factors of -20	$-1, 20$	$1, -20$	$-2, 10$	$2, -10$	$-4, 5$	$4, -5$
Sum of factors $(m + n)$	19	-19	8	-8	1	-1

The table shows that the values of m and n you want are $m = -4$ and $n = 5$.
So, $x^2 + x - 20 = (x - 4)(x + 5)$.

Factor.

10. $x^2 + 4x - 12$ **11.** $x^2 + 4x - 45$ **12.** $x^2 + x - 56$

Mixed Review

State the inverse.

13. Add -16. **14.** Subtract 35. **15.** Divide by $\frac{2}{3}$.

Solve the inequality.

16. $x + 9 < 16$ **17.** $-6x \geq 36$ **18.** $\frac{x}{7} > -5$

19. *Find the Numbers* The sum of two numbers is 34. The second
number is two more than the first. Find the two numbers.

Algebra 2
Basic Skills Workbook: Diagnosis and Remediation

NAME _____ DATE _____

Quick Check

Review of Topic 5, Lesson 1

Standardized Testing Quick Check

1. Which expression is the greatest common factor of $-8x^3$ and $36x^5$?

   A. $-x^3$

   B. $4x^3$

   C. $(4x^3)(-2 + 9x^2)$

   D. $8x^2$

2. What is the correct factorization of $36x^4 - 60x^3$?

   A. $-6x^3(6x + 10)$

   B. $6x^3(6x - 10)$

   C. $12x^3(3x - 5)$

   D. $12x^2(3x^2 - 5x)$

Homework Review Quick Check

Find the greatest common factor and factor it out of the expression.

3. $24x^4 - 9x$ **4.** $32x^5 + 12x^3$

5. $18x^2 - 27x^6$ **6.** $15x^2y^4 - 33x^4y^2$

NAME _____ DATE _____

Practice

For use with Lesson 5.2: Factoring $x^2 + bx + c$

Match the trinomial with the correct factorization.

1. $x^2 + x - 12$ **A.** $(x + 4)(x + 3)$

2. $x^2 + 7x + 12$ **B.** $(x - 4)(x - 3)$

3. $x^2 - 7x + 12$ **C.** $(x + 4)(x - 3)$

4. $x^2 - x - 12$ **D.** $(x - 4)(x + 3)$

Choose the correct factorization. If neither is correct, find the correct factorization.

5. $x^2 + 14x + 48$ 6. $x^2 - 3x - 10$ 7. $x^2 + 8x - 33$

A. $(x + 6)(x + 8)$ **A.** $(x - 2)(x + 5)$ **A.** $(x + 3)(x - 11)$

B. $(x + 4)(x + 12)$ **B.** $(x - 5)(x + 2)$ **B.** $(x - 3)(x - 11)$

Factor the trinomial.

8. $x^2 + 8x - 9$ 9. $x^2 - 10x + 21$ 10. $x^2 + 5x - 24$

11. $x^2 + 13x + 36$ 12. $x^2 - 3x - 18$ 13. $x^2 + 14x + 40$

14. $x^2 - x - 56$ 15. $x^2 - 7x - 30$ 16. $x^2 + 12x + 32$

17. $x^2 + 3x - 54$ 18. $x^2 - 2x - 15$ 19. $x^2 - 20x + 100$

20. $x^2 + 2x - 63$ 21. $x^2 - 10x - 24$ 22. $x^2 + 16x + 39$

23. $x^2 + 6x - 55$ 24. $x^2 - 9x - 70$ 25. $x^2 - 22x + 40$

Algebra 2
Basic Skills Workbook: Diagnosis and Remediation

NAME _____ DATE _____

Factoring $ax^2 + bx + c$

GOAL **Factor quadratic expressions of the form $ax^2 + bx + c$.**

Understanding the Main Ideas

In this lesson, you will learn how to factor quadratic polynomials whose leading coefficient is not 1. To do this, find the factors of a *(m and n)* and the factors of c *(p and q)* so that the sum of the outer and inner products *(mq and pn)* is b.

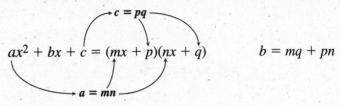

$$ax^2 + bx + c = (mx + p)(nx + q) \qquad b = mq + pn$$

with $c = pq$ and $a = mn$

Example: $6x^2 + 22x + 20 = (3x + 5)(2x + 4) \qquad 22 = (3 \cdot 4) + (5 \cdot 2)$

with $20 = 5 \cdot 4$ and $6 = 3 \cdot 2$

Once you determine the factors of a and c, it is necessary to test them to see which produces the correct factorization. In Example 1, there is only one pair of factors for a and c.

EXAMPLE 1

Factor $2x^2 + 5x + 3$.

SOLUTION

Test the possible factors of a (1 and 2) and c (1 and 3).

Try $a = 1 \cdot 2$ and $c = 3 \cdot 1$.

$\qquad (1x + 3)(2x + 1) = 2x^2 + 7x + 3 \qquad$ Not correct

Now try $a = 1 \cdot 2$ and $c = 1 \cdot 3$.

$\qquad (1x + 1)(2x + 3) = 2x^2 + 5x + 3 \qquad$ Correct

The correct factorization of $2x^2 + 5x + 3$ is $(x + 1)(2x + 3)$.

Factor the expression.

  1. $3x^2 + 2x - 1$ **2.** $2x^2 + 11x + 5$ **3.** $5x^2 + 8x + 3$

For more complicated expressions like that in Example 2 and Example 3 where there are several pairs of factors for a and c, it is convenient to set up a table when testing the factors.

(continued)

NAME _____ DATE _____

Factoring $ax^2 + bx + c$

EXAMPLE 2

Factor $2x^2 - 3x - 5$.

SOLUTION

Factors of a and c	Product	Correct?
$a = 1 \cdot 2$ and $c = (-1)(5)$	$(x - 1)(2x + 5) = 2x^2 + 3x - 5$	No
$a = 1 \cdot 2$ and $c = (5)(-1)$	$(x + 5)(2x - 1) = 2x^2 + 9x - 5$	No
$a = 1 \cdot 2$ and $c = (1)(-5)$	$(x + 1)(2x - 5) = 2x^2 - 3x - 5$	Yes
$a = 1 \cdot 2$ and $c = (-5)(1)$	$(x - 5)(2x + 1) = 2x^2 - 9x - 5$	No

The correct factorization of $2x^2 - 3x - 5$ is $(x + 1)(2x - 5)$.

Factor the expression.

4. $3x^2 - 4x - 7$ **5.** $5x^2 - 14x - 3$ **6.** $7x^2 + 13x - 2$

EXAMPLE 3

Factor $8x^2 - 26x + 15$.

SOLUTION

Both factors of c must be negative, because b is negative and c is positive. Test the possible factors of a and c.

Factors of a and c	Product	Correct?
$a = 1 \cdot 8$ and $c = (-15)(-1)$	$(x - 15)(8x - 1) = 8x^2 - 121x + 15$	No
$a = 1 \cdot 8$ and $c = (-1)(-15)$	$(x - 1)(8x - 15) = 8x^2 - 23x + 15$	No
$a = 1 \cdot 8$ and $c = (-3)(-5)$	$(x - 3)(8x - 5) = 8x^2 - 29x + 15$	No
$a = 1 \cdot 8$ and $c = (-5)(-3)$	$(x - 5)(8x - 3) = 8x^2 - 43x + 15$	No
$a = 2 \cdot 4$ and $c = (-15)(-1)$	$(2x - 15)(4x - 1) = 8x^2 - 62x + 15$	No
$a = 2 \cdot 4$ and $c = (-1)(-15)$	$(2x - 1)(4x - 15) = 8x^2 - 34x + 15$	No
$a = 2 \cdot 4$ and $c = (-3)(-5)$	$(2x - 3)(4x - 5) = 8x^2 - 22x + 15$	No
$a = 2 \cdot 4$ and $c = (-5)(-3)$	$(2x - 5)(4x - 3) = 8x^2 - 26x + 15$	Yes

The correct factorization of $8x^2 - 26x + 15$ is $(4x - 3)(2x - 5)$.

Factor the expression.

7. $4x^2 - 12x + 9$ **8.** $8x^2 - 26x + 21$ **9.** $9x^2 + 18x - 16$

If a, b, and c have a common factor, factor out the common factor before testing the possible factors of a and c, as shown in Example 4.

(continued)

Algebra 2
Basic Skills Workbook: Diagnosis and Remediation

NAME _____ DATE _____

Factoring ax² + bx + c

EXAMPLE 4

Factor $6x^2 - 2x - 8$.

SOLUTION

Begin by factoring out the common factor 2.

$$6x^2 - 2x - 8 = 2(3x^2 - x - 4)$$

Now factor $3x^2 - x - 4$ by testing the possible factors of a and c.

Factors of *a* and *c*	Product	Correct?
$a = 1 \cdot 3$ and $c = (-1)(4)$	$(x - 1)(3x + 4) = 3x^2 + x - 4$	No
$a = 1 \cdot 3$ and $c = (4)(-1)$	$(x + 4)(3x - 1) = 3x^2 + 11x - 4$	No
$a = 1 \cdot 3$ and $c = (1)(-4)$	$(x + 1)(3x - 4) = 3x^2 - x - 4$	Yes
$a = 1 \cdot 3$ and $c = (-4)(1)$	$(x - 4)(3x + 1) = 3x^2 - 11x - 4$	No
$a = 1 \cdot 3$ and $c = (-2)(2)$	$(x - 2)(3x + 2) = 3x^2 - 4x - 4$	No
$a = 1 \cdot 3$ and $c = (2)(-2)$	$(x + 2)(3x - 2) = 3x^2 + 4x - 4$	No

The correct factorization is $6x^2 - 2x - 8 = 2(x + 1)(3x - 4)$.

Factor the expression.

10. $4x^2 - 16x + 16$ **11.** $8x^2 + 22x + 12$ **12.** $8x^2 + 20x + 8$

Mixed Review

Find the slope and *y*-intercept of the graph of the equation.

13. $y = -8x + 3$ **14.** $y - 6x = 13$ **15.** $y = \frac{2}{3}x - 9$

16. Plot the quadrilateral with vertices $A(-4, 6)$, $B(2, 10)$, $C(2, 1)$, and $D(-7, -3)$ in a coordinate plane.

NAME _____ DATE _____

Quick Check

Review of Topic 5, Lesson 2

Standardized Testing Quick Check

1. Which is the correct factorization of $x^2 - 5x - 24$?

    A. $(x - 8)(x + 3)$

    B. $(x + 8)(x - 3)$

    C. $(x - 6)(x + 4)$

    D. $(x + 6)(x - 4)$

2. Which is the correct factorization of $x^2 + 15x - 54$?

    A. $(x + 6)(x - 9)$

    B. $(x + 18)(x - 3)$

    C. $(x + 6)(x + 9)$

    D. $(x - 18)(x + 3)$

Homework Review Quick Check

Factor the trinomial.

3. $x^2 - 13x + 40$ **4.** $x^2 + 15x + 54$ **5.** $x^2 + 6x - 40$

Algebra 2
Basic Skills Workbook: Diagnosis and Remediation

NAME _____ DATE _____

Practice

For use with Lesson 5.3: Factoring $ax^2 + bx + c$

Match the trinomial with the correct factorization.

1. $3x^2 + 14x + 8$ **A.** $(3x - 2)(x + 4)$

2. $3x^2 - 23x - 8$ **B.** $(3x + 1)(x - 8)$

3. $3x^2 + 23x - 8$ **C.** $(3x + 2)(x + 4)$

4. $3x^2 + 10x - 8$ **D.** $(3x - 1)(x + 8)$

Choose the correct factorization. If neither is correct, find the correct factorization.

5. $3x^2 + 7x - 6$ 6. $6x^2 - 7x - 3$ 7. $4x^2 - 21x + 5$

  A. $(3x - 1)(x + 6)$ **A.** $(3x - 1)(2x - 3)$ **A.** $(4x - 1)(x - 5)$

  B. $(3x - 2)(x + 3)$ **B.** $(6x - 1)(x + 3)$ **B.** $(2x - 1)(2x - 5)$

Factor the trinomial.

8. $2x^2 + 9x + 7$ 9. $3x^2 - 8x - 16$ 10. $4x^2 - 16x + 15$

11. $5x^2 + 12x - 9$ 12. $4x^2 + 11x + 6$ 13. $6x^2 - 23x + 20$

14. $6x^2 - 3x - 3$ 15. $8x^2 + 42x - 36$ 16. $7x^2 + 33x - 10$

17. $4x^2 - 10x - 14$ 18. $4x^2 + 24x + 35$ 19. $9x^2 - 12x - 12$

20. $5x^2 + 41x - 36$ 21. $6x^2 + 3x - 30$ 22. $7x^2 - 59x - 36$

23. $4x^2 + 37x + 40$ 24. $10x^2 - 27x + 18$ 25. $8x^2 + 26x + 21$

NAME _____ DATE _____

Factoring Special Cases

GOAL Use special product patterns to factor quadratic polynomials.

Terms to Know	Example/Illustration
Prime factor a factor that cannot be factored using integer coefficients	$x^2 + 5x + 6 = (x + 3)(x + 2)$ Prime factors
Factoring a polynomial completely to write a polynomial as the product of: • monomial factors • prime factors with at least two terms	$2x^2 - 8 = 2(x^2 - 4)$ $= 2(x - 2)(x + 2)$

Understanding the Main Ideas

When factoring quadratic polynomials, it is helpful to be able to recognize special product patterns.

Factoring Special Products

Difference of Two Squares Pattern
$a^2 - b^2 = (a + b)(a - b)$

Example:
$9x^2 - 4 = (3x + 2)(3x - 2)$

Perfect Square Trinomial Pattern
$a^2 + 2ab + b^2 = (a + b)^2$
$a^2 - 2ab + b^2 = (a - b)^2$

Example:
$x^2 + 10x + 25 = (x + 5)^2$
$x^2 - 14x + 49 = (x - 7)^2$

EXAMPLE 1

Factor the difference of two squares.

  a. $x^2 - 9$ **b.** $4x^2 - 36$ **c.** $48 - 75x^2$

SOLUTION

a. $x^2 - 9 = x^2 - 3^2$ Write as $a^2 - b^2$.
         $= (x + 3)(x - 3)$ Factor using pattern.

b. $4x^2 - 36 = (2x)^2 - 6^2$ Write as $a^2 - b^2$.
            $= (2x + 6)(2x - 6)$ Factor using pattern.

c. $48 - 75x^2 = 3(16 - 25x^2)$ Factor out common factor.
             $= 3[4^2 - (5x)^2]$ Write as $a^2 - b^2$.
             $= 3(4 + 5x)(4 - 5x)$ Factor using pattern.

(continued)

Factoring Special Cases

Factor.

1. $49 - x^2$ **2.** $81 - 100x^2$ **3.** $15x^2 - 60$

EXAMPLE 2

Factor each perfect square trinomial.

a. $x^2 - 6x + 9$ **b.** $25x^2 + 20x + 4$ **c.** $5x^2 - 20x + 20$

SOLUTION

a. $x^2 - 6x + 9 = x^2 - 2(x)(3) + 3^2$ Write as $a^2 - 2ab + b^2$.
$\quad\quad\quad\quad\quad\quad = (x - 3)^2$ Factor using pattern.

b. $25x^2 + 20x + 4 = (5x)^2 + 2(5x)(2) + 2^2$ Write as $a^2 + 2ab + b^2$.
$\quad\quad\quad\quad\quad\quad\quad = (5x + 2)^2$ Factor using pattern.

c. $5x^2 - 20x + 20 = 5(x^2 - 4x + 4)$ Factor out common factor.
$\quad\quad\quad\quad\quad\quad = 5[x^2 - 2(x)(2) + 2^2]$ Write as $a^2 - 2ab + b^2$.
$\quad\quad\quad\quad\quad\quad = 5(x - 2)^2$ Factor using pattern.

Factor.

4. $x^2 - 12x + 36$ **5.** $3x^2 + 42x + 147$ **6.** $9x^2 - 6x + 1$

You can use the distributive property to help you factor a polynomial completely.
To factor a polynomial completely, write it as the product of monomial factors
and prime factors with at least two factors.

EXAMPLE 3

Factor $3x^3 + 15x^2 + 12x$.

SOLUTION

$3x^3 + 15x^2 + 12x = 3x(x^2 + 5x + 4)$ Factor out common monomial factor.
$\quad\quad\quad\quad\quad\quad = 3x(x + 1)(x + 4)$ Factor completely.

Factor completely.

7. $9x^3 - 6x^2 + x$ **8.** $2x^3 - 24x^2 + 72x$ **9.** $4x^3 + 16x^2 + 16x$

You can use the distributive property to factor a polynomial with four terms.
Sometimes you can factor the polynomial by grouping into two groups of terms
and factoring the greatest common factor out of each term.

(continued)

NAME _____ DATE _____

Factoring Special Cases

EXAMPLE 4

Factor each polynomial completely.

   a. $x^3 + 2x^2 + 3x + 6$ **b.** $x^3 + 3x^2 - 4x - 12$

SOLUTION

a. $\begin{aligned} x^3 + 2x^2 + 3x + 6 &= (x^3 + 2x^2) + (3x + 6) \\ &= x^2(x + 2) + 3(x + 2) \\ &= (x + 2)(x^2 + 3) \end{aligned}$ Group terms.
     Factor each group.
     Use distributive property.

b. $\begin{aligned} x^3 + 3x^2 - 4x - 12 &= (x^3 + 3x^2) - (4x + 12) \\ &= x^2(x + 3) - 4(x + 3) \\ &= (x + 3)(x^2 - 4) \\ &= (x + 3)(x + 2)(x - 2) \end{aligned}$ Group terms.
     Factor each group.
     Use distributive property.
     Factor difference of squares.

Factor completely.

10. $x^3 + 6x^2 - 9x - 54$ **11.** $x^3 - x^2 - 16x + 16$

Mixed Review

Simplify the radical expression.

12. $\sqrt{98}$ **13.** $\sqrt{108} \cdot \sqrt{56}$ **14.** $\sqrt{\dfrac{12}{25}}$

15. *Geometry*   The surface area of a sphere is given by $4\pi r^2$, where r is the radius and π is approximately 3.14. What is the surface area of the sphere at the right in terms of b?

5b

NAME _____ DATE _____

Quick Check

Review of Topic 5, Lesson 3

Standardized Testing Quick Check

1. Which one of the following is a correct factorization of the expression $-16x^2 + 36x + 52$?

   A. $(-16x + 26)(x - 2)$

   B. $(-4x - 13)(4x + 4)$

   C. $-1(4x - 13)(4x + 4)$

   D. $-1(4x - 4)(4x + 13)$

Homework Review Quick Check

Match the trinomial with the correct factorization.

2. $15x^2 + 11x - 12$ **A.** $(5x + 4)(3x - 3)$

3. $15x^2 - 3x - 12$ **B.** $(5x - 2)(3x + 6)$

4. $15x^2 + 24x - 12$ **C.** $(5x - 3)(3x + 4)$

5. $15x^2 + 8x - 12$ **D.** $(5x + 6)(3x - 2)$

NAME _____ DATE _____

Practice

For use with Lesson 5.4: Factoring Special Cases

Factor the expression.

1. $x^2 - 9$ **2.** $64x^2 - 100$ **3.** $6x^2 - 150$

4. $12x^2 - 75$ **5.** $36 - 121x^2$ **6.** $98 - 18x^2$

7. $x^2 - y^2$ **8.** $4x^2 - 25y^2$ **9.** $72x^2 - 162y^2$

Factor the expression.

10. $x^2 - 2x + 1$ **11.** $x^2 + 8x + 16$

12. $x^2 + 30x + 225$ **13.** $4x^2 + 4x + 1$

14. $9x^2 - 24x + 16$ **15.** $3x^2 - 36x + 108$

16. $9x^2 + 6x + 1$ **17.** $18x^2 + 12x + 2$

18. $36x^2 - 84x + 49$ **19.** $25x^2 - 20x + 4$

20. $18x^2 - 60x + 50$ **21.** $25x^2 + 70x + 49$

Factor the expression. Tell which special product factoring pattern you used.

22. $x^2 - 25$ **23.** $x^2 + 18x + 81$

24. $25x^2 - 49$ **25.** $32 - 18x^2$

26. $2x^2 - 40x + 200$ **27.** $-2x^2 + 36x - 162$

28. $196 - 4x^2$ **29.** $-192 + 147x^2$

30. $x^2 + x + \frac{1}{4}$ **31.** $32x^2 - 162y^2$

Factor the expression completely.

32. $-7x^3 + 28x^2 - 21x$ **33.** $3x^3 - 12x$

34. $-2x^4 - 12x^3 - 18x^2$ **35.** $4x^4 + 16x^3 - 20x^2$

36. $18x^3 - 288x$ **37.** $-9x^4 + 24x^3 - 16x^2$

38. $50x^3 + 160x^2 + 128x$ **39.** $18x^3 - 33x^2 - 30x$

40. $x^4 + x^3 - 12x - 12$ **41.** $x^3 - 3x^2 + x - 3$

42. $6x^4 + 5x^3 - 24x - 20$ **43.** $3x^3 - x^2 - 21x + 7$

Algebra 2
Basic Skills Workbook: Diagnosis and Remediation